WHSmith

Revise

Science

KS3: YEAR 7

Age 11–12

Mark Levesley

First published in 2007
exclusively for WHSmith by
Hodder Murray, a member of the Hodder Headline group
338 Euston Road
London
NW1 3BH

Impression number 10 9 8 7 6 5 4 3 2 1
Year 2011 2010 2009 2008 2007

A CIP record for this book is available from the British Library.

Cover illustration by Sally Newton Illustrations

Typeset by GreenGate Publishing Services, Tonbridge, Kent
Illustrations by Barking Dog Art

ISBN-13: 978 0 340 94295 6

Printed and bound in Italy

Contents

Parents' guide

This series provides the very best available help for your child in tackling the demands of learning and revising the material in Key Stage 3 Science.

Each book is a valuable resource to have at home to support your child's school science work throughout the three years of Key Stage 3. Each is also a fantastic revision guide, providing a clear and concise set of revision notes combined with strategies for maximising revision efficiency.

Features

- follows the teaching order of the majority of school science courses
- has questions on every page
- answers to Practice questions are provided so children can learn from their mistakes
- activities to do
- fascinating facts to add interest

Active learning and revision strategies

Learning and revision are active processes! It's very easy to sit down and read something for half an hour and then think 'I've revised that'. However, we all know from experience how easy it is to realise 'I haven't a clue what I've been reading for the last 5 minutes'. To stop this happening, and to make the most of learning and revision time, this book continually challenges children with activities and questions, helping them to remain active in their thoughts. The book also teaches children a variety of revision strategies – proven ways that make it easier to remember things.

What can you do to help?

Revision can't be done by parents or guardians! However, you can help by taking an interest in your child's work, and some children will want you to test them. The Practice questions, with their answers, make this easy to do. As a challenge, ask one of the questions that appear at the start of each double page – these need longer, more detailed answers. All the information a child needs for their longer answers is in the units.

A bit of background

Key Stage 3 is from about age 11 to age 14 (Years 7–9). During this period of your child's education there are various compulsory subjects, of which science is one. At the end of Key Stage 3 your child will be tested using SATs (Standard Attainment Tests) in Science, Maths and English. The results from SATs are given as 'Levels' and most children are expected to attain a 'Level 6'. Some children may have progressed further, attaining a 'Level 7'. This book covers the material needed for all levels from 3 to 7.

Units in this book

The material that your child needs to learn for science is set out in the National Curriculum. The order in which this material is studied is left up to individual schools. However, the vast majority of published science courses use the 'QCA Scheme of Work' as their basis. This Scheme of Work divides science into 12 topics that are studied in each year. This book gives two units to each of these topics from the Scheme of Work, so that you can easily use it alongside most modern school textbooks.

Learner's guide

What is learning?

Learning is 'getting things to stick in your memory'. Sometimes this is easy and sometimes it's tricky. In this book you'll meet various ways to help you learn things.

The golden rule of learning is that 'it is an active process'. You actually have to concentrate and *do* something rather than just reading.

Use a separate file or exercise book to make your notes and diagrams, and to answer the questions.

Using each unit

Each unit starts with some questions in a green panel. These are the key questions that the unit will help you answer. See how much you already know by trying to answer the questions before you work through the unit.

Then try the 'Get started' question, outlined in blue. This is an open-ended question, but you can check your answer on pages 56–61.

Now read through and learn the information in the unit. The words in **bold** are important words you should know. Their meanings can be found in the glossary at the back of the book.

Finally, answer the numbered Practice questions and check your answers thoroughly.

Once you have finished a unit, tick off the 'How did I do?' questions, to confirm you can now answer the key questions more fully.

Ways of remembering things

Throughout the book you'll find boxes like these:

> A concept map is a series of words and phrases with lines between them to show links. You can write on the lines what the links are.

> **FACT**
> About 8 million blood cells die in your body every second.

These boxes describe ways to help you remember things and give you interesting facts that help you to learn more about a topic. Try out the different ideas and you'll find that some work better for you than others. Once you've found the ways that work for you, use them for other things that you need to learn.

Here are some memory strategies to try:

Mnemonics

Pronounced '*nem-**on**-icks*', these are silly words or phrases that can help you remember the order of things in a list. For instance, the colours of the rainbow are red, orange, yellow, green, blue, indigo, violet. One mnemonic is a boy's name: ROY G BIV. Or you can use a silly sentence where the first letter of each word is the first letter of the word you need to remember: **R**ichard **O**f **Y**ork **G**ave **B**attle **I**n **V**ain.

Altered words

Misspell or mispronounce words on purpose to remember things (e.g. 'bears hi*bear*nate').

Links

Make up sentences where there are links between letters (e.g. *B*ee stings are treated with *B*icarbonate of soda).

Saying out loud

Some people remember things better if they say them out loud. Doing this for all your revision might get a bit annoying (especially for those listening), so just try it with an important sentence or two – and try using a silly voice or doing an impression of someone.

Rhymes

Make up a silly rhyme (e.g. Righty Tighty – you turn taps to the right to tighten them).

Flow charts and drawings

Draw a silly picture...

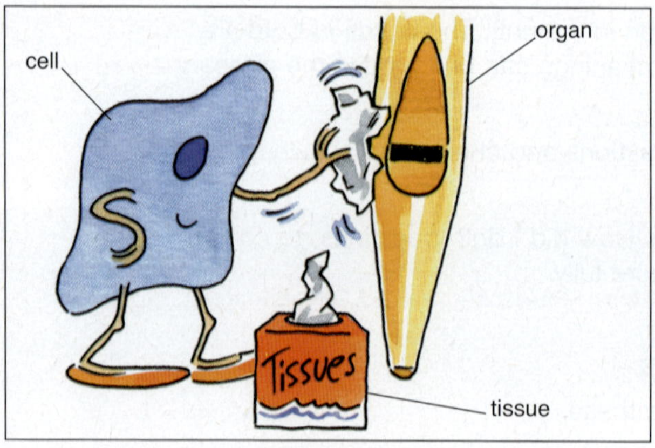

...or a flow chart.

Mental images

Create strange images in your mind. For instance, to remember that fish have scales think of a fish sitting on a set of scales.

Concept maps

Many people like to summarise their revision using concept maps. These take a bit of practice. They start with an important word or phrase in the middle and then other words and phrases are linked in, until you end up with a web showing all the links between many words and phrases. Adding drawings to a concept map really helps. Concept maps can be very large. Here's an example.

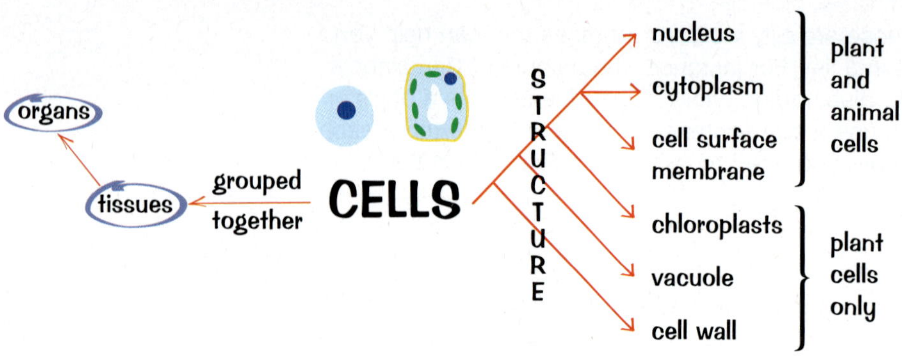

Repetition

Doing things over and over again is more likely to make them stick in your mind. It might be saying a sentence over and over, or doing any of the other things listed earlier. Repeating things is a very good way of memorising them.

Learning and your brain

The more recently a path through a forest has been used, the more obvious it is and the easier it is to follow. If the path is used often, it will be very easy to follow. If the path is lined with blue trees it will be even easier to follow! It's the same with memories. There are paths in your brain that lead to your memories. When you remember something you use a path. The things that you are most likely to remember are things that you learned recently, things that you repeated to yourself and learned again and again, and things that stick out. To get things to stick out use one of the ways of learning listed in the previous section!

A place in a forest is more likely to be found if there are more paths to it. If you learn a piece of information in different ways, you create different paths to that information. Use more than one way of learning each thing you need to remember.

Planning your revision

When it comes to revising:

- start early – well before an exam or test
- plan *what* you are going to do and *when* you are going to do it, and stick to the plan
- do a small amount at a time (say 20 minutes) and then have a break (say 5 minutes)
- don't have any distractions (TV, radio and iPods are generally not helpful)
- always *do* something as you revise (say things out loud, write things down, imagine things)
- you should aim to finish a revision session with some brief notes about what you have revised. Write these notes on cards. Later the same day look through the cards again to remind yourself of what you've learned. This is a really good, simple way of getting information to stick. And you can keep the cards to refer to again and again.

1: Cells

In this unit you will learn to answer these questions:

- What are living organisms made from?
- How is a microscope used to view cells?
- What are cells like?

Get started

Your **heart** is an **organ** that pumps blood. Write a list of as many human organs and their **functions** as you can. Check your answers on page 56. Add the ones you missed to your list.

Plants have organs too. **Leaves** make food, **roots** take in water and hold a plant in place, **stems** provide support and **flowers** are used to make seeds.

FACT About 8 million blood cells die in your body every second.

All organs are made of **tissues**. Your heart contains muscle tissue and fat tissue. And tissues are made of **cells**. Muscle tissue is made of muscle cells and fat tissue is made of fat cells.

Just as buildings are made of bricks, so animals and plants are made of cells. You need a **microscope** to see these cells because they are so small. Microscopes **magnify** things.

A microscope

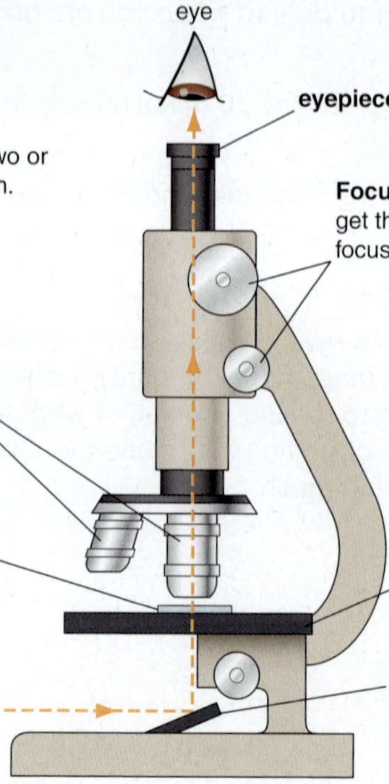

Practice

1. Make a list of all the words in bold type on this page. Look at the Glossary and make sure you can say to yourself what each word means. Go through your list again and again until you get it all correct.
2. A microscope has a ×10 eyepiece lens and a ×20 objective lens. What is its magnifying power?
3. What does a coverslip do?

Cells found in animals look different from cells found in plants. Plant cells are more 'boxy' looking but both types of cells share some parts that are the same.

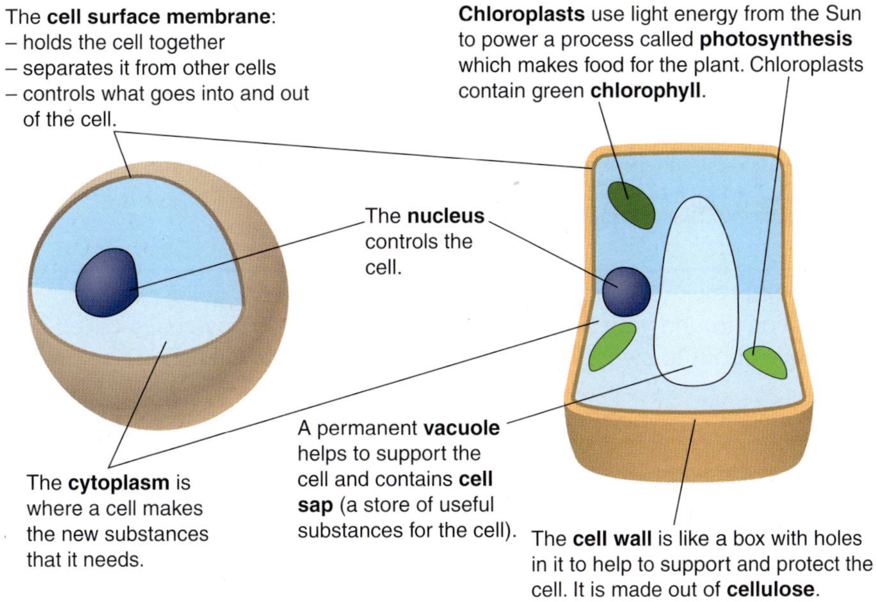

An animal cell (left) and a plant cell (right)

Look at page 5 to see what a mnemonic is. A mnemonic for plant cell parts is: My New Computer Comes With Viruses. Write out the mnemonic and look at the diagram on the left to find the words that it helps you to remember.

4 Make up a mnemonic for human organs.

5 What does a nucleus do?

6 State two functions of the cell wall.

7 Which parts of a plant cell can you also find in an animal cell?

8 a Copy and complete this drawing of a cell and label all its parts.

b Does your drawing show an animal or a plant cell? How do you know?

9 Which word is the odd one out and why?

cell chloroplast organ tissue

10 Draw a picture of yourself at the very start of your life. Label your picture.

FACT You started off your life as one cell, smaller than a full stop.

How did I do?

	✔
I know what living organisms are made from.	☐
I know how a microscope is used to view cells.	☐
I know what cells are like.	☐

2: What cells do

In this unit you will learn to answer these questions:

- What do cells do?
- How are new cells made?
- What causes pollen tubes to grow?

Get started

Sperm cells swim towards **egg cells**. **Neurones** (**nerve cells**) carry information around your body. **Ciliated epithelial cells** have hairs called **cilia** that wave about to sweep things along. What cells are A, B and C below?

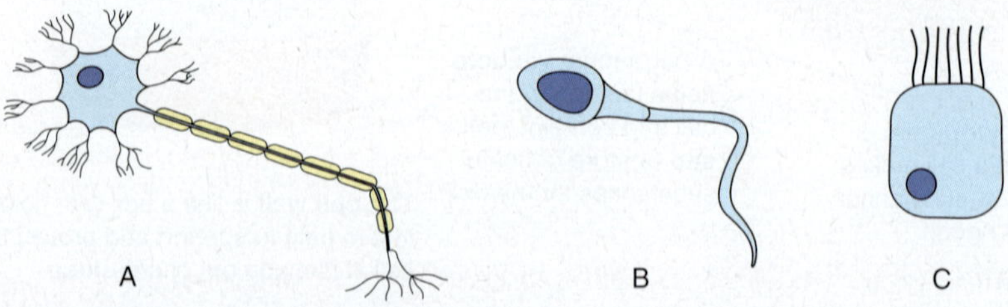

FACT The longest neurone in an adult is about 1.3 metres long and carries information between the foot and the spine.

Cells have differences depending on their functions – cells are **adapted** to their functions. A neurone is long so that it can carry information a long way. Muscle cells can change length. A plant **root hair cell** has a bit sticking out of it that provides more area for water to get into the cell. These cells can quickly take water out of the ground.

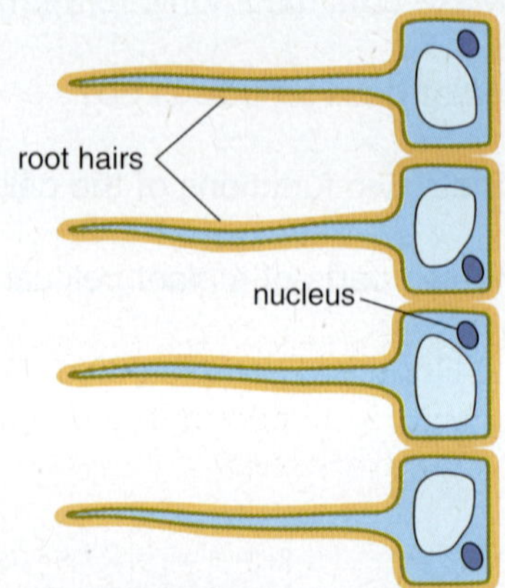

Root hair tissue

Cells of the same type form a tissue. Lots of muscle cells form **muscle tissue**. Lots of root hair cells together are called **root hair tissue**.

When an **organism** (living thing) grows, its cells increase in number and get bigger. Cells increase in number by **cell division**.

Remember diagrams by drawing them from memory. Shut the book and draw cell division. Keep drawing it until you can get it all correct.

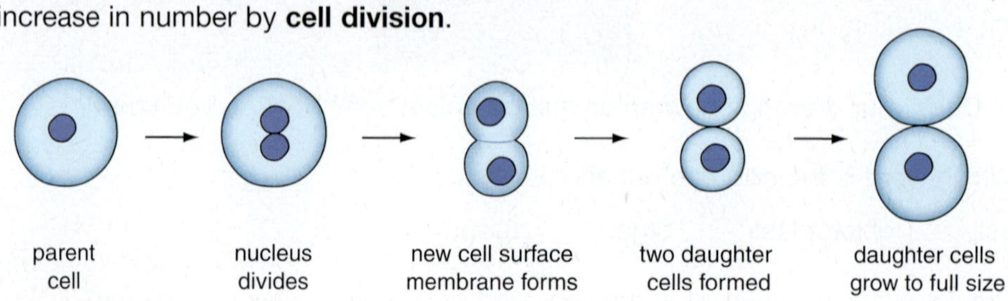

Cell division

Practice

1. What is a tissue?
2. In which plant organ would you find root hair tissue?
3. How do organisms grow?
4. How are neurones adapted to their function?

Sex cells are used to create new organisms (**reproduction**). Plant sex cells are **pollen grains** (male) and **egg cells** (female).

First, a pollen grain from one flower is carried to the **stigma** of another flower by insects or the wind. This is **pollination**. A pollen grain grows a **pollen tube** through the **style** and down to the **ovule** (which contains the egg cell). The nucleus from the pollen grain joins with the egg cell nucleus in a process called **fertilisation**, and a **fertilised egg cell** is formed. This will form the **embryo** of the **seed** and grow into a new plant.

The new nucleus formed in fertilisation contains all the instructions needed to make a new plant.

The **stigmas** of flowers contain sugar, which pollen grains need to grow a pollen tube. The amount of sugar affects how many pollen tubes will grow. In an experiment, six groups of 100 pollen grains were added to water containing different amounts of sugar. The bar chart shows the results of the experiment.

Lots of pollen grains were used in the experiment – a big **sample size**. If only a few pollen grains were used, it would be difficult to see the effect of the sugar since some pollen grains will never grow and one or two will always grow. Using a bigger sample size gives you stronger evidence.

Draw a flow chart to show the stages in making a fertilised egg cell.

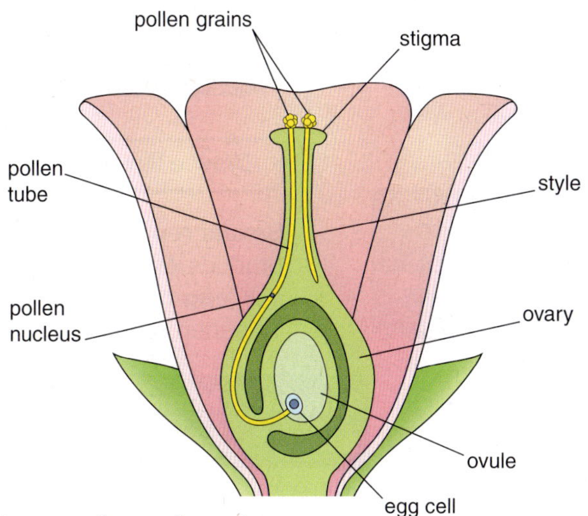

How a pollen grain nucleus reaches an egg cell in a flower

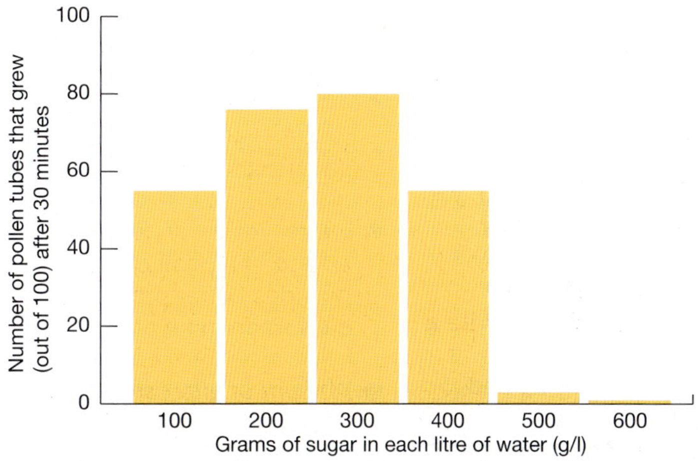

5 a In the experiment, what conditions allowed the most pollen tubes to grow?

b Write a title for the **bar chart** on the right.

c Why is it important to use a large sample size?

6 a Draw and label a root hair cell.

b How is it adapted to its function?

7 What tissue is this?

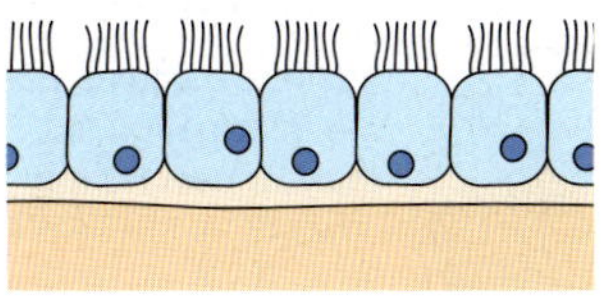

FACT Saffron is a yellow spice made from the dried stigmas of a crocus.

8 One cell becomes four cells. Draw a diagram to show how this happens.

How did I do?

	✔
I know what cells do.	☐
I know how new cells are made.	☐
I know what causes pollen tubes to grow.	☐

3: Reproduction

In this unit you will learn to answer these questions:

- How does a new life start?
- When can human fertilisation take place?

Get started

Draw a flow chart to show the stages that happen to produce a human baby.

FACT Sperm cells swim at about 15 cm per hour.

Sexual reproduction is the process by which male and female organisms produce **offspring**. In animals, a male **sex cell** (**sperm cell**) and a female sex cell (**egg cell**) **fuse** together (**fertilisation**) and produce a **fertilised egg cell**. This then grows into a new organism.

Type of animal	Number of egg cells produced at one time	Type of fertilisation	Type of development	Amount of aftercare
fish	millions	external	external	none
frog	thousands	external	external	none
bird	1–6	internal	external	months
human	usually 1	internal	internal	years

- *Internal/external fertilisation* – fertilisation occurs inside the female or outside (e.g. in water). Sex cells are more likely to meet each other inside a female so animals using internal fertilisation produce fewer egg cells.
- *Internal/external development* – the **embryo** grows outside the mother (e.g. an egg in a nest) or inside (e.g. in a woman's **uterus**). Internal development provides better protection and so an animal needs to produce fewer egg cells since more embryos are likely to survive.
- *Amount of aftercare* – how long an animal looks after its offspring. The more aftercare, the fewer egg cells an animal needs to produce.

Count how many points you need to remember about sex cell adaptations in the diagram below. Write a list from memory. Check your list and write it out again.

Sperm cells and egg cells are adapted to their functions.

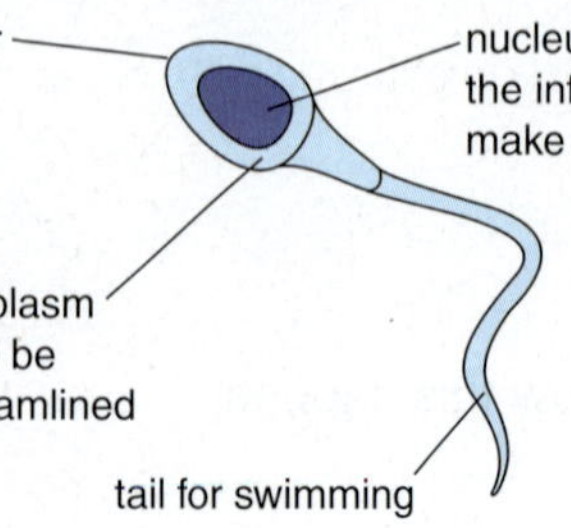

A human sperm cell is 0.06 mm long.

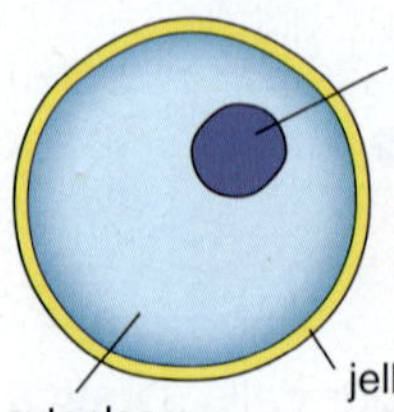

A human egg cell is 0.1 mm wide.

Practice

1. Why do ducks produce fewer egg cells than goldfish?
2. Where does a human embryo develop?

Sperm cells are made in the **testes** of the **male reproductive system**. Egg cells are made in the **ovaries** of the **female reproductive system**.

Male reproductive system

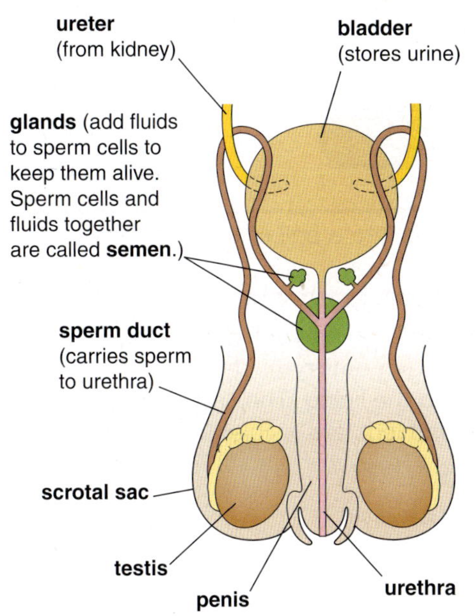

Female reproductive system

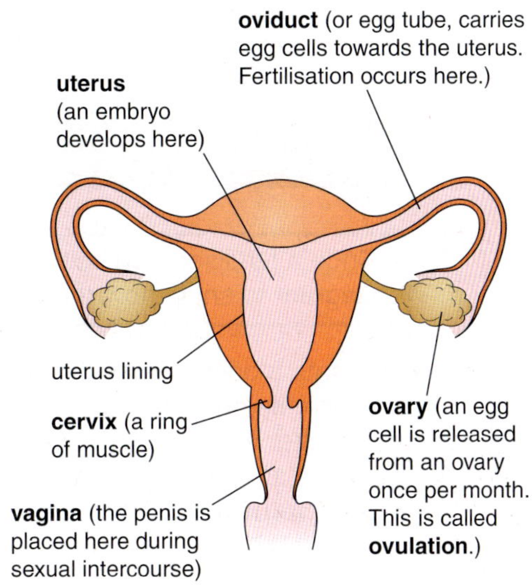

The lining of the uterus breaks apart each month and passes out of the vagina. This is called **menstruation** (a period). The lining then regrows and this makes sure that an embryo has a fresh lining. This monthly cycle is called the **menstrual cycle** and varies slightly in length between different women.

Think up two mnemonics for the names of the parts of the male and female reproductive systems.

3 Tracey's menstrual cycle lasts 28 days.

a How many egg cells does she produce in 3 months?

b She starts to menstruate on 30 September. When is her next menstruation due?

c What happens during menstruation?

d Why does this happen?

4 Where are sperm cells produced?

5 These muddled words are parts of the male or female reproductive systems. Unmuddle the words and say what each part does.

a SUTURE b SCRUM DEPT c VOID CUT

FACT

A man's testes produce about 1000 sperm cells per second.

How did I do?

	✔
I know how a new life starts.	☐
I know when human fertilisation can take place.	☐

4: Growing up

In this unit you will learn to answer these questions:
- How is the human fetus supported as it develops?
- What do newborn babies need?
- How do humans change as they grow?

Get started

Once a fertilised egg cell is formed it turns into a ball of cells. Draw a diagram to show how this happens.

FACT Fingerprints form about 8 weeks before birth.

Fertilisation occurs in an oviduct and the fertilised egg cell divides by cell division (see page 10) to form a ball of cells (an **embryo**). This reaches the uterus after about 3 days and **implants** into the lining. The embryo grows and a **placenta** and **amnion** form. When arms and legs are visible the embryo is called a **fetus** (pronounced '***fee**-tus*').

A fetus in the uterus

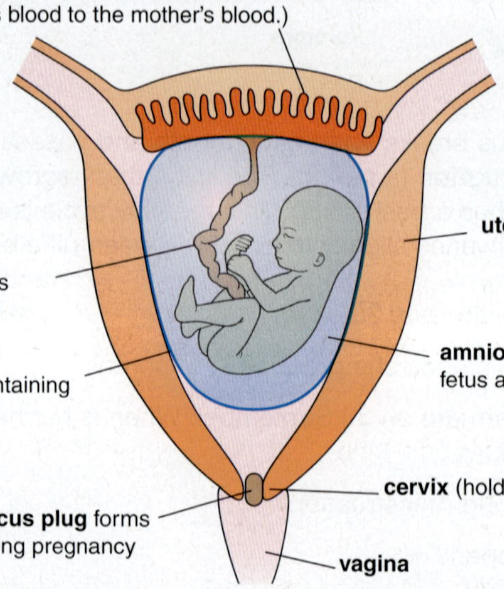

Draw and label a diagram to show what happens at the placenta. Start your diagram like this:

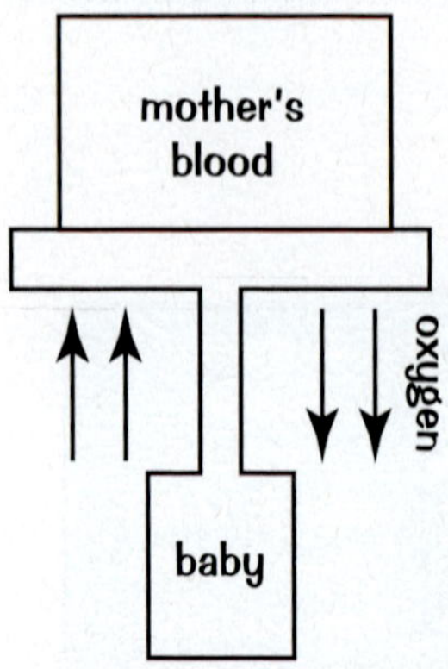

Alcohol, chemicals in cigarette smoke and some viruses (e.g. rubella) pass through the placenta and can harm the baby or cause it to be born early (**premature**). Usually the baby is ready to be born after 9 months (the **gestation** period). The cervix gets wider and the uterus **contracts** (gets smaller), pushing the baby out head first. After the baby is born the placenta is pushed out (the **afterbirth**).

A new baby has no teeth and is fed milk to give it all the **nutrients** it needs to grow. Human breast milk contains **antibodies** that help to stop the baby getting diseases.

Practice

1. Why is a new baby given milk?
2. How is a baby pushed out of the mother?

A baby grows bigger as its cells divide. The baby grows into a child, then an adolescent and then an adult. **Adolescence** is the time when big emotional and physical changes occur in you. The physical changes occur during a period called **puberty**.

The changes at puberty are caused by **hormones** – chemicals that are made in your body and travel in your blood.

Draw out a time line from fertilised egg cell to adult. Label your time line with notes about what happens at each stage in the human life cycle.

The physical changes in males and females that occur during puberty

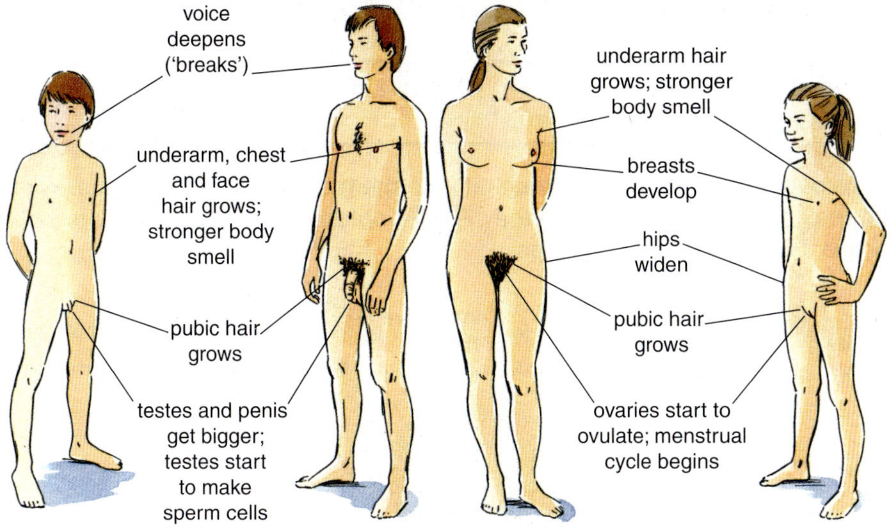

During puberty people grow much taller but different people enter puberty at different times. If you measured the height of every 12-year-old in the UK, you would find that, on average, girls who are 12 years and 6 months old are taller than those who are just 12. If you used a smaller **sample size** (e.g. girls in your school) you may not find this. Bigger sample sizes provide more reliable evidence.

FACT Robert Wadlow (1918–1940) was 2.72 m tall – the tallest person ever.

3 Write down a list of ways in which you have changed in the last 2 years.

4 Write another list of ways in which you will change in the next 2 years.

5 Oxygen gets into a mother in her lungs. Describe the route of oxygen from her lungs to her developing fetus's brain.

6 a What are hormones?

b What can they do?

7 Part of a letter in a newspaper reads: 'Both my children are taller than me, so I know that all children are taller than their parents'. Why is this piece of evidence not very reliable?

How did I do?

	✔
I know how the human fetus is supported as it develops.	☐
I know what newborn babies need.	☐
I know how humans change as they grow.	☐

5: Habitats

In this unit you will learn to answer these questions:

- How does the environment influence the animals and plants living in a habitat?
- How do environments vary?

Get started

Write a list of organisms that live underground. Can you identify one feature that all these organisms have?

Animals and plants have features that help them to live in certain areas. We say that they are **adapted** to where they live. Adaptations help organisms to survive. Here are some examples:

Swordfish live in an ocean habitat

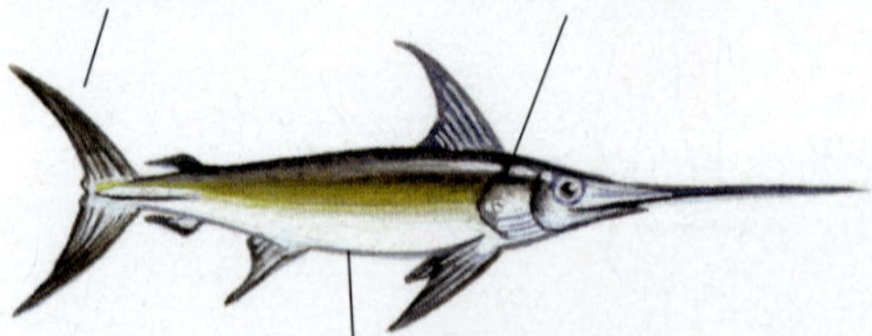

Camels live in deserts

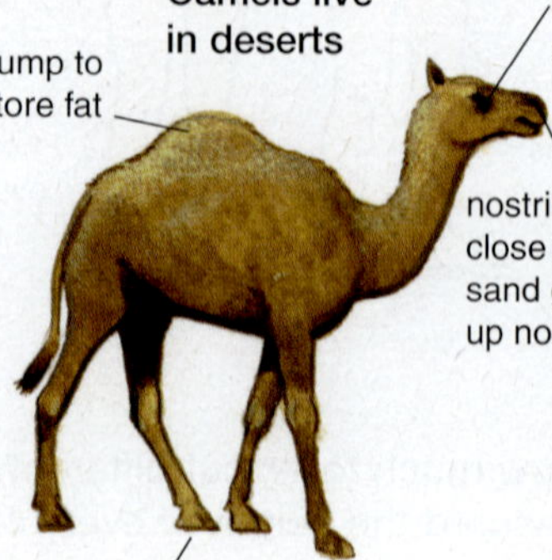

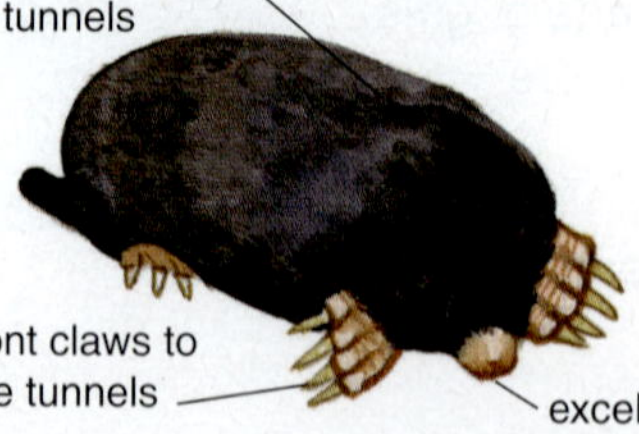

Moles live underground

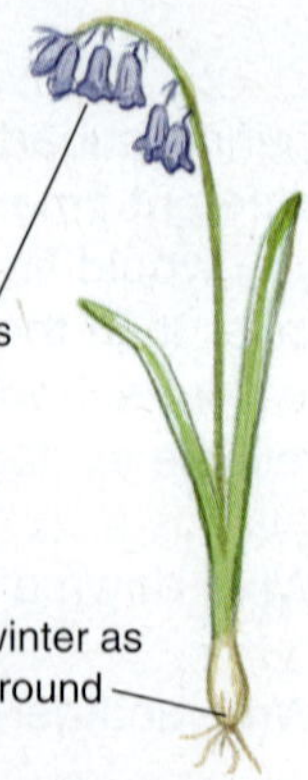

Bluebells live in woods

The place where an organism lives is its **habitat**. What it's like in a habitat is known as the **environment**. The environment of a habitat is caused by **physical environmental factors** (e.g. amount of light, temperature, wetness). Different organisms are found in different places in a habitat due to differences in environments.

FACT

In 1620, when Admiral Beaulieu saw penguins, he thought they were feathered fish because they were so well adapted to living underwater.

Practice

1. Design and draw an animal that is adapted to live in the Arctic. Label your drawing.
2. Describe the environment in a desert habitat.
3. Many desert animals are the colour of sand. Why might this be a good adaptation?
4. Write a list of all the habitats mentioned on this page.

The environment in a habitat can change during a day. For example, it's light during the day and dark at night. These are **daily changes**. Organisms are adapted to daily changes.

You can remember an example of an animal that hibernates by using: 'bears hi*bear*nate'.

Many owls sleep in the day and come out at night (they are **nocturnal**).

Sea anemones close up when the tide goes out so they don't dry out.

Ecologists are scientists who investigate habitats. They ask questions (for example: Where do dormice go when it gets dark? Do moss plants prefer dry or damp places?). Then they plan investigations, making sure that they only change one thing. So, if they are investigating how light affects woodlice, they keep everything the same (temperature, moisture, number of woodlice) and only change the amount of light. This is a **fair test**. They also make sure they use large sample sizes.

Habitats also change during the course of a year (for example, it is hot in summer and cold in winter). These are **seasonal changes**.

Arctic hares turn white in winter. This helps them to be camouflaged against the snow.

Hedgehogs eat a lot in the autumn and go to sleep (**hibernate**) in the winter when there is not much food around. Many plants stay below ground in winter (as bulbs) and trees lose their leaves because a lot of the water they need may be frozen.

Swallows leave the UK for the winter and go to South Africa where it is warm and there is plenty of food. This is called **migration**.

5 What is the difference between a daily change and a seasonal change?

6 a A deer grows thicker hair in winter. What sort of change is this?

b Why is this a useful adaptation?

7 Why do some animals hibernate?

8 Name one animal that migrates.

9 What is a fair test?

FACT Swallows fly about 16 000 km each year as they migrate. They can travel up to 300 km in a day.

How did I do?

	✔
I know how the environment influences the animals and plants living in a habitat.	☐
I know how environments vary.	☐

6: Feeding relationships

In this unit you will learn to answer these questions:

- What is a feeding relationship?
- What do food webs tell us?

Get started

Draw a diagram to show that foxes eat rabbits and that rabbits eat grass.

An animal that eats other animals is called a **predator**. The animals it eats are its **prey**. Predators have adaptations to allow them to catch and eat their prey. Examples include:

- forward-facing eyes for good three dimensional (3D) vision
- sharp claws to grab with
- sharp teeth or beaks to rip flesh apart.

Prey animals have adaptations to help stop them being eaten. Examples include:

- excellent senses of sight, smell and hearing
- eyes on the sides of the head for all-round vision
- armour, horns or camouflage.

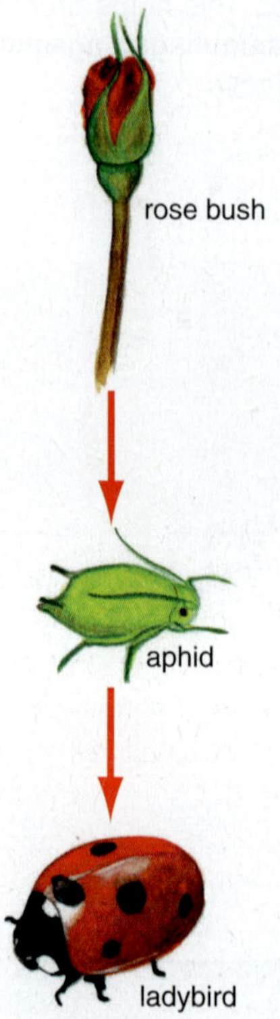

A food chain

A **food chain** shows what eats what. The arrows show where energy goes. For example, in the food chain shown on the left, energy goes from the rose bush to the aphid because aphids eat rose bushes.

There are lots of other words you need to know:

- A **producer** is an organism that makes its own food (for example a plant).
- A **carnivore** eats other animals.
- A **herbivore** eats plants.
- A **consumer** eats other organisms.

Practice

1. What adaptations does a lion have for being a predator?
2. Write out the food chain shown above and write down whether each organism is a predator, carnivore, herbivore, etc.

FACT Cheetahs use speed to help them catch their prey. They can run at 70 mph.

Organisms in a habitat feed on each other. We say that there are **feeding relationships** in a habitat and we show these using a **food web**. A food web is lots of food chains all joined together.

The food web below is from a hedge habitat (even in a small habitat there are lots of different organisms).

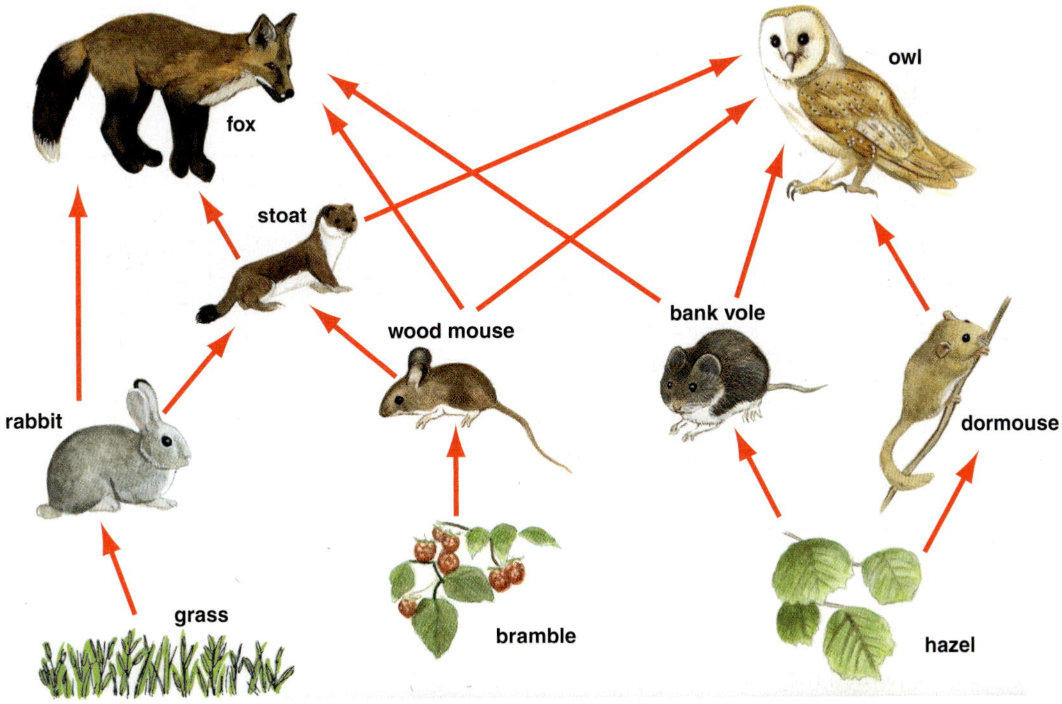

Scientists search for evidence in habitats to tell them what eats what. They watch animals, search for their tracks, and examine bite marks and droppings.

Many animals that are prey try to avoid being eaten! And some plants do too. Stinging nettles, for example, will sting animals on their noses.

The number of organisms of one type in a habitat is called a **population**. If you change the population of an organism it will affect the populations of other organisms in a food web. For instance, if all the brambles in a hedge are removed, the numbers of wood mice will go down because there's nothing for them to eat.

To think about changes in a food web, imagine that the arrows are pieces of string. Imagine tugging on the string connected to one organism and thinking about which other organisms will be able to feel this tugging.

3 Look at the food web above. Write down a food chain from the web with four organisms in it.

4 What do the arrows in a food web show?

5 What do owls eat?

6 Rose bushes are eaten by aphids. Hedgehogs eat earthworms and ladybirds (which like to eat aphids). Earthworms eat dead leaves. Draw a food web to show these feeding relationships.

7 a In the food web above, what would happen if all the hazel trees died?
b What would happen if there was a sudden increase in the number of rabbits?

8 Why don't rabbits eat stinging nettles?

FACT Chillis contain chemicals that make them too hot for many animals to eat. Many humans love to put them in cooking!

How did I do?

	✔
I know what a feeding relationship is.	☐
I know what food webs tell us.	☐

7: Variation

In this unit you will learn to answer these questions:

- How do individuals of the same species differ from each other?
- What are the causes of variation?

Get started

How are these two animals different from each other? List all the ways.

FACT Sometimes members of different species can breed but their offspring are not able to. Lions and tigers can produce ligers.

Organisms look different – we call this **variation**. There is variation between different **species** (for example lions and tigers) and there is variation between members of the same species (for example, humans all look different).

Scientists take measurements to compare one organism with another. You may have taken measurements like this at school (such as height, arm span, hand width, arm length). Scientists ask questions to investigate variation, such as: Are blond-haired people shorter than brown-haired people?

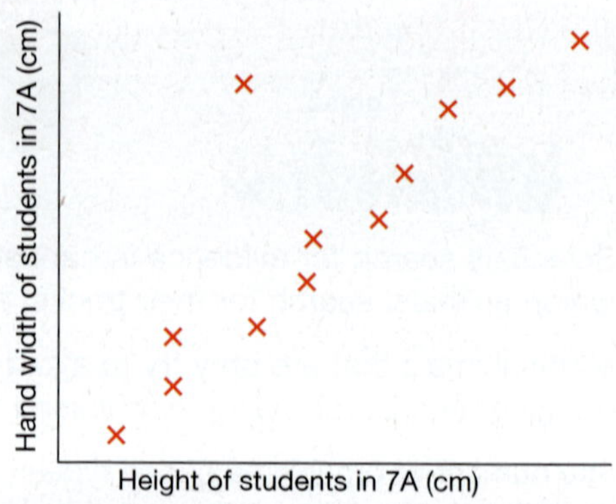

Scatter graph to compare hand width and height of students in 7A

Bar chart to compare height and hair colour of students in 7A

The **data** are best displayed in a graph or a chart. You usually use a **line graph** or a **scatter graph** when *all* your measurements are numbers.

The scatter graph shows that, *generally,* taller people do have wider hands. We say that there is a strong **correlation**.

Practice

1. What is variation?
2. List three ways in which you are different to one of your teachers.
3. a What question do you think the scientists who drew the scatter graph asked?

   b What correlation does the scatter graph show?
4. Does the bar chart show a correlation?

You will often find that children share similar **characteristics** with their parents. This is because some characteristics are **inherited** – they are passed from parents to children. In the family below you can see that Katie has inherited her dimpled chin from her dad.

Mum and Dad are not related to each other and so don't look alike, but Richard and Katie have inherited characteristics from each parent. The variation caused by inheriting characteristics is called **inherited variation**.

Inherited characteristics include things like eye colour, skin colour, a dimpled chin, lobed ears, hair colour and hair curliness.

Plants also have inherited characteristics, like leaf shape and flower colour.

However, our surroundings and what we do also affect our characteristics. Scars, sunburn and hair length are all examples of **environmental variation**. You also find environmental variation in plants (for instance height, colour of leaves).

Many characteristics are due to a mixture of inherited variation *and* environmental variation. Height is an example.

5 Who has Katie inherited her hair colour and type from?

6 A plant is not very tall. Write down as many reasons as you can think of why this might be.

7 Which is the odd one out and why?

sunburn hair length eye colour scar

8 Draw a picture of yourself. Label all the examples of environmental variation down the left of your portrait. Label all the examples of inherited variation down the right.

FACT The sex of some animals is an example of environmental variation. Alligator eggs kept below 30 °C will be female, those kept above 34 °C will be male.

Writing lists with headings and subheadings is a good way of learning things. Write lists of characteristics caused by inherited variation, environmental variation and by both.

How did I do?

	✔
I know how individuals of the same species differ from each other.	☐
I know what the causes of variation are.	☐

8: Classification

In this unit you will learn to answer these questions:

- How can we describe living things?
- How can we sort things into groups?
- How do scientists classify living things?

Get started

Write a list of similarities and differences between these two animals. What one characteristic is the best for telling these animals apart?

Scientists like to have names for organisms and to be able to tell them apart. The naming of organisms, based on what they look like and what they do, is called **classification**.

The drawing on the right shows a honey bee and the labels show the sorts of things that scientists look at when they are observing animals. All **insects** have three body parts and six legs, which is how you can tell them apart from **arachnids**, which have two body parts and eight legs.

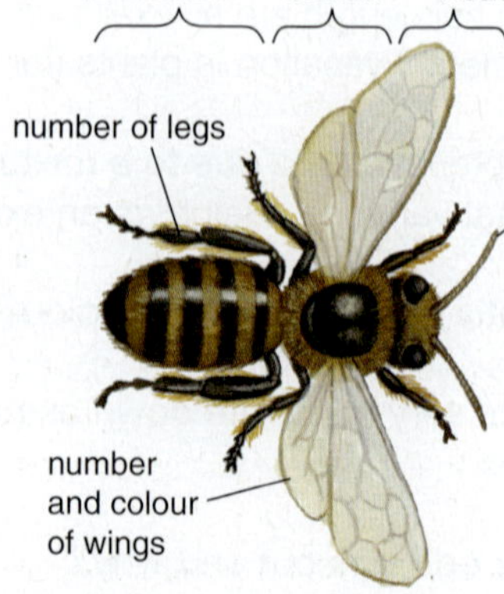

Honey bee

FACT There are about 20 000 different species of bee!

Using their observations, scientists have divided all organisms into a number of large groups called **kingdoms**. The two biggest kingdoms are the plant kingdom and the animal kingdom.

Practice

1. a The drawing on the right shows a bumble bee. How can you tell that it is an insect?

   b How can you tell it apart from a honey bee?

2. What are kingdoms?

The animal kingdom can be divided into two groups – **vertebrates** (animals with backbones) and **invertebrates** (animals without backbones). These groups can then be divided into more groups. The diagram shows the characteristics of the different groups.

The groups of vertebrates can be remembered using a mnemonic: MR FAB.

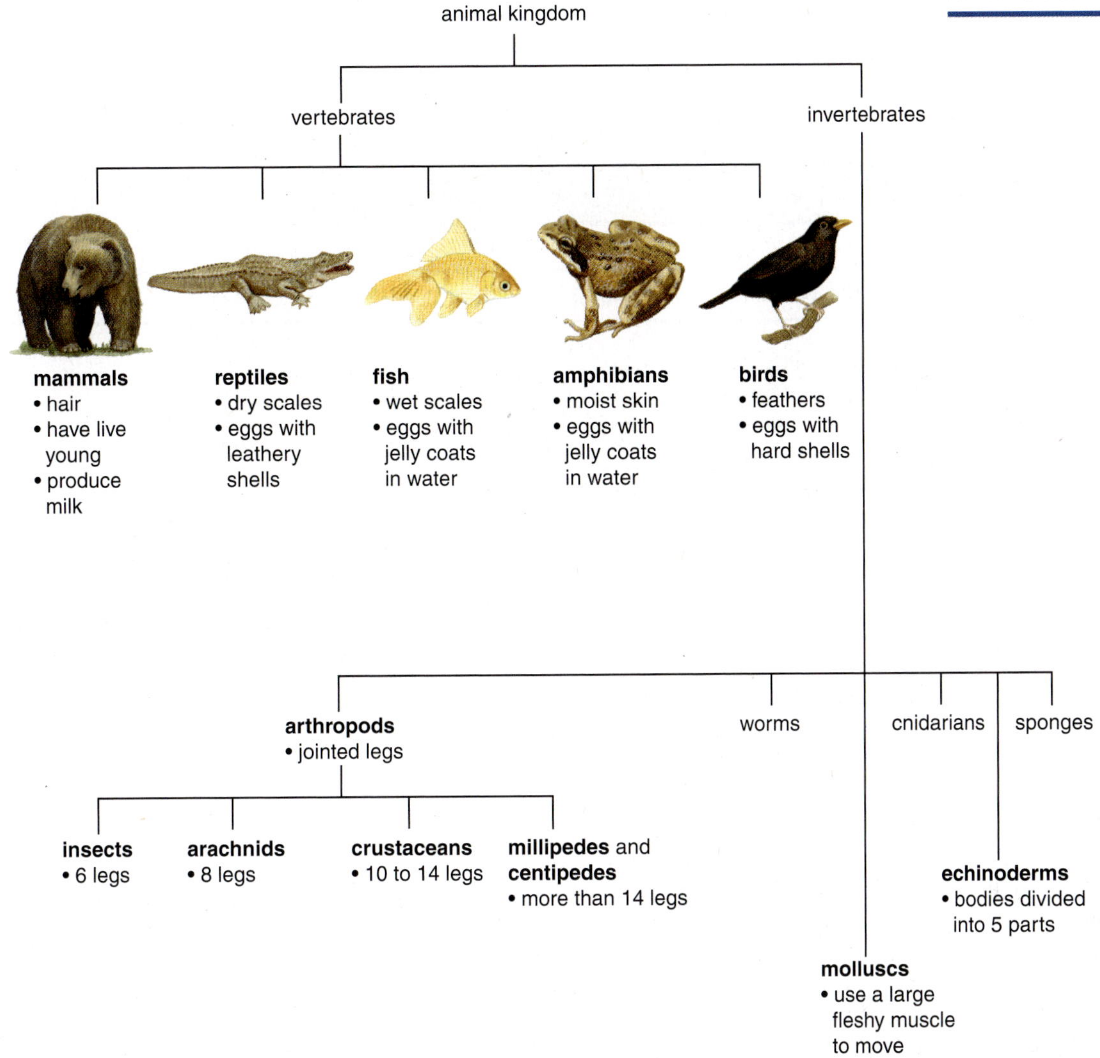

3. What is the best characteristic to use to divide vertebrates into their different groups?

4. How are arthropods sorted into groups?

5. List all the groups that a bumble bee is in.

6. Make a large version of the diagram above using a word processing program on a computer. You could find some pictures of the different animals on the internet and add them to your diagram.

FACT

Amphibians can take oxygen out of the air or water through their skin. They have lungs too.

How did I do?

	✔
I know how we describe living things.	☐
I know how we can sort things into groups.	☐
I know how scientists classify living things.	☐

9: Acids and alkalis

In this unit you will learn to answer these questions:
- What are acids and alkalis like and where do we use them?
- How can acids and alkalis be identified and distinguished from each other?
- Is there a range of acidity and alkalinity?

Get started

Make two lists – what acids are like and what alkalis are like.

Acids are liquids that have a sour taste, although it is very dangerous to taste some acids! The drawings show some common acids.

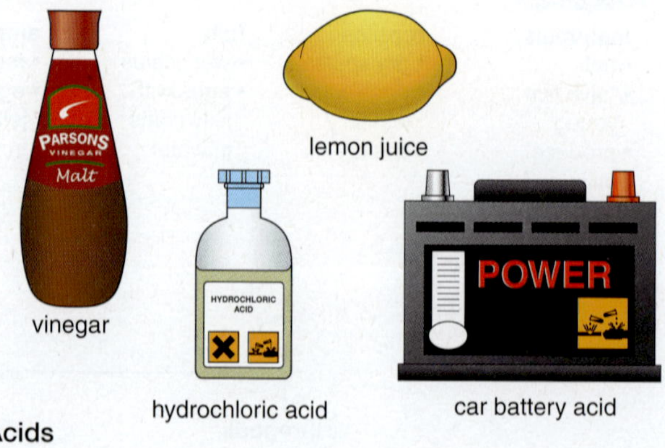

Acids

Alkalis

Alkalis are liquids that have a soapy feel, although it is very dangerous to touch some alkalis. The drawings show some common alkalis.

Many acids and alkalis are clear and colourless and look like water. The harmful ones have **hazard symbols** on their containers.

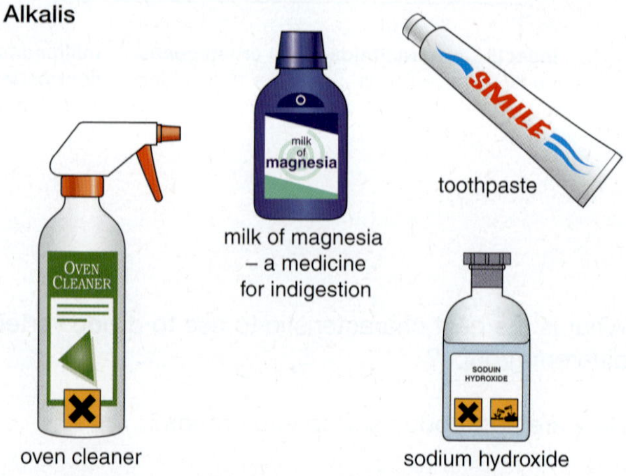

To make some acids and alkalis safer, you can add water. This is called **dilution**. The acids and alkalis that you use in the school lab are diluted so that they are no longer corrosive.

Hazard symbols

Harmful or **irritant** – the substance will hurt you if swallowed, splashed on your skin or into your eyes.

Corrosive – the substance attacks skin and causes severe damage.

Flammable – the substance catches fire easily.

FACT Turkey vulture urine contains a strong acid. The birds urinate on their legs to kill bacteria!

Practice

1. Name two dangerous acids.
2. If you spill a strong acid you should add water to it before mopping it up. Why?
3. Design your own hazard symbol for poisonous substances. Check the answers to see how your answer compares with the real one.

Some parts of plants contain dyes that turn different colours in acids and alkalis. The dye from **litmus** moss is a purple colour. If acid is added to litmus it turns red. If an alkali is added it turns blue. Adding pure water doesn't change its colour.

Remember the mnemonic RABAL: Reds are Acids, Blues are Alkalis.

Dyes that do this are called indicators. Other indicators include beetroot juice and red cabbage juice.

FACT Hydrangea plants have blue flowers when grown in acidic soils and red flowers when grown in alkaline soils.

Some substances are neither acid nor alkali and so don't change the colour of an indicator. Substances like this are **neutral**. Pure water is neutral.

Lots of indicators mixed together make **universal indicator**, which has a range of colours to show how strong an acid or an alkali is. The strengths are measured on the **pH scale** – 0 is the strongest acid and 14 is the strongest alkali.

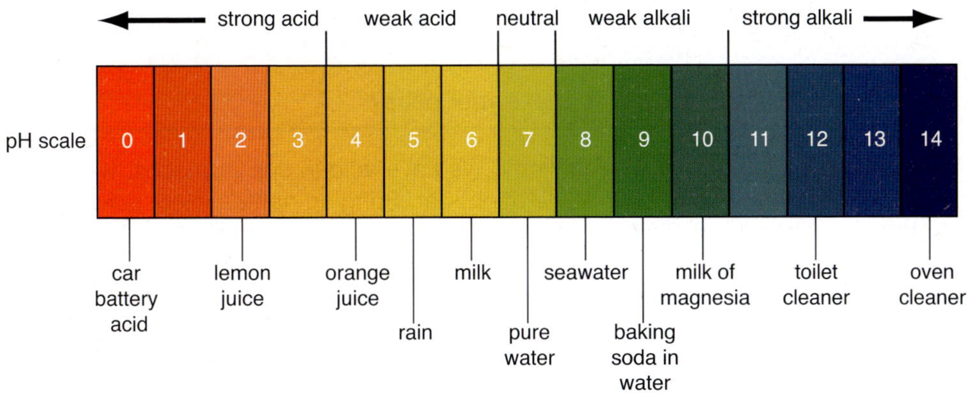

The colours of universal indicator and the pH scale

4 Vinegar has a pH between that of lemon juice and orange juice. What is the pH of vinegar?

5 Is orange juice a strong or a weak acid?

6 Name a strong alkali.

7 What is an indicator?

8 a What pH do neutral liquids have?

b Name one neutral liquid.

9 What colour does pure water turn:

a litmus

b universal indicator?

10 Make a copy of the pH scale above and find out the pHs of some more liquids to add to it.

How did I do?

	✔
I know what acids and alkalis are like and where we use them.	☐
I know how acids and alkalis can be identified and distinguished from each other.	☐
I know there is a range of acidity and alkalinity.	☐

10: Neutralisation

In this unit you will learn to answer these questions:

- What happens when an acid is added to an alkali?
- Where is neutralisation important?

Get started

Sort these acids and alkalis into pairs of opposites.

car battery acid	milk	milk of magnesia
orange juice	oven cleaner	seawater

How did you decide on how to make your pairs?

FACT Your body uses neutralisation to keep the pH of your blood between 7.35 and 7.45.

Acids and alkalis are used by organisms. We have acid in our stomachs, which helps to kill harmful microbes that we might eat. Stinging nettles inject acids into the skin when touched. Many insect bites contain acids or alkalis.

Wasp stings are alkaline. We can make a wasp sting feel better by putting an acid on it, such as vinegar. Sometimes there's too much acid in your stomach (called indigestion or heartburn). **Antacid** tablets contain a weak alkali and are used to treat this. Soils that are too acidic to grow certain crops can be made less acidic by adding an alkali, and vice versa.

Inventing a silly sentence can help you to remember things. '*B*ee stings are treated with *B*icarbonate of soda and *V*asp stings are treated with *V*inegar'. (All said in a silly accent!)

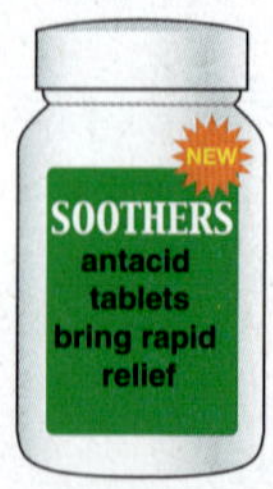

When an alkali is added to an acid, the pH of the acid rises towards pH 7. When an acid is added to an alkali, the pH of the alkali falls towards pH 7. Since pH 7 is neutral, we call this process **neutralisation**.

Practice

1. What is neutralisation?
2. How would you neutralise an acidic soil?
3. Why do antacids contain a weak alkali and not a strong one?
4. Are bee stings acidic or alkaline? How did you work out your answer?

A class wanted to find out which of four antacid tablets was best. They measured out 150 cm^3 of hydrochloric acid (stomach acid) and added universal indicator. The acid had a pH of 2. Then they added powdered antacid until the pH was over 6. They repeated this with all four antacids and recorded the amount of antacid needed each time. The bar chart shows their results.

FACT The Romans used ground-up coral as an antacid. This contains calcium carbonate, which is still used in some antacids today.

Bar chart to show how much antacid is needed to raise the pH of hydrochloric acid to over pH 6, for four different antacids

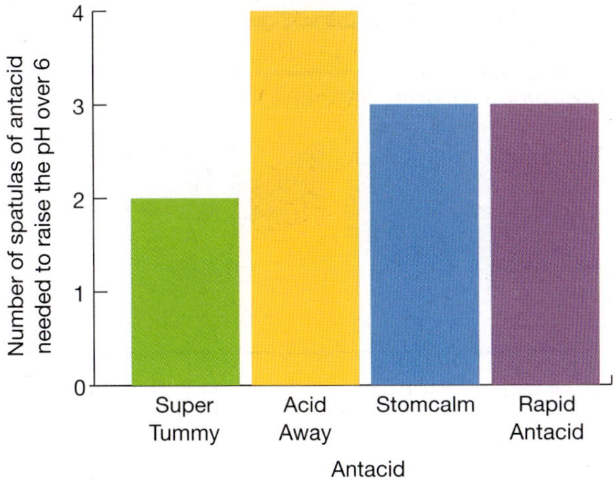

The class used a small spoon called a spatula to measure out the antacid. This was a fair test because they used the same type and amount of acid each time. The only thing they changed was the type of antacid.

5 Which was the best antacid? How do you know?

6 Write down a list of all the apparatus (equipment) that the group would have used for its investigation.

7 Think up some different questions about antacids that you could investigate. Think about how quickly they work or how much antacid different tablets contain.

A concept map is a series of words and phrases with lines between them to show links. You can write on the lines what the links are.

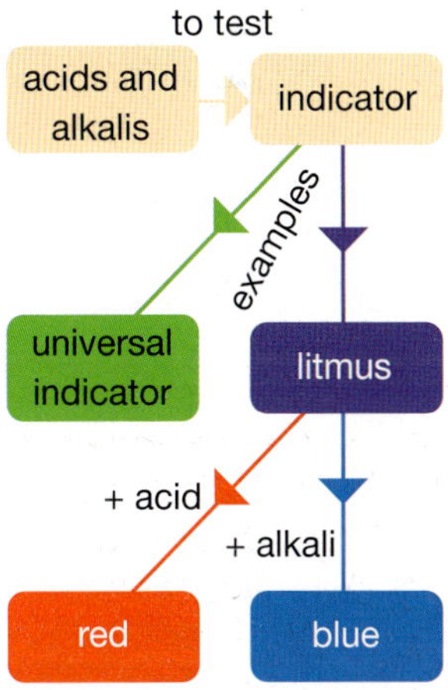

There's no right or wrong way to draw a concept map but it helps to make it colourful and to add little drawings. Try drawing a concept map using all the words in bold type on pages 24 to 27. Use the map shown here as a starting point.

How did I do?

	✔
I know what happens when an acid is added to an alkali.	☐
I know where neutralisation is important.	☐

11: Simple chemical reactions

In this unit you will learn to answer these questions:

- What is a chemical reaction?
- How do acids react with metals?
- How do acids react with carbonates?

Get started

What's the difference between what happens in these two diagrams?

When ice melts it doesn't change substance – it's still water and you can turn it back into ice. This is a **physical change** since no new substances are formed. It is also a **reversible change** because you can reverse it!

When an egg is fried, the yolk and the white change colour. New substances form and so this is a **chemical reaction**. It is also an **irreversible change** because you can't change the cooked egg back into raw egg.

In a chemical reaction new substances are formed. Things that tell you a chemical reaction is happening include: changes of colour, bubbles of gas, the substances getting hot or a flame appearing.

In a chemical reaction, you start with **reactants** and you end with **products**.

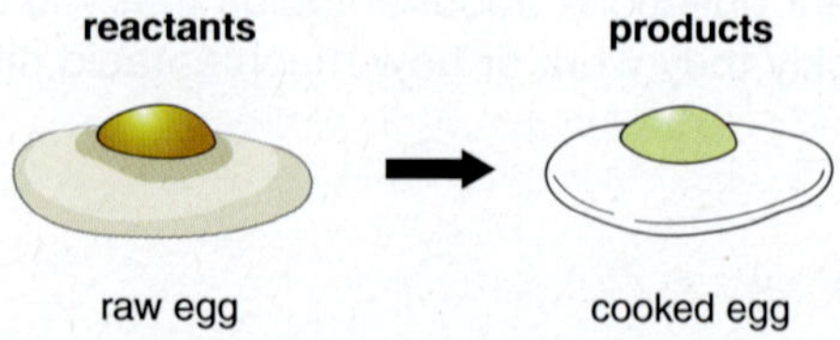

FACT The reaction between hydrogen and oxygen is used in rockets.

Some reactions need help to get started. If you mix hydrogen gas with oxygen nothing happens. If you put a flame to them, they explode with a squeak.

Some reactions don't need help to get started. If you mix carbon dioxide gas with **limewater**, the limewater goes milky.

Practice

1. What is the difference between a chemical reaction and a physical change?
2. When you add hydrochloric acid to calcium metal, the metal bubbles. Why?
3. Which of these is the odd one out and why?

   water → steam   potato → crisp   wood → ash   bread → toast

When a strip of magnesium metal is dropped into an acid, bubbles appear. Eventually the metal disappears. A chemical reaction has occurred in which the acid has **corroded** the metal. Many metals react with acids in this way.

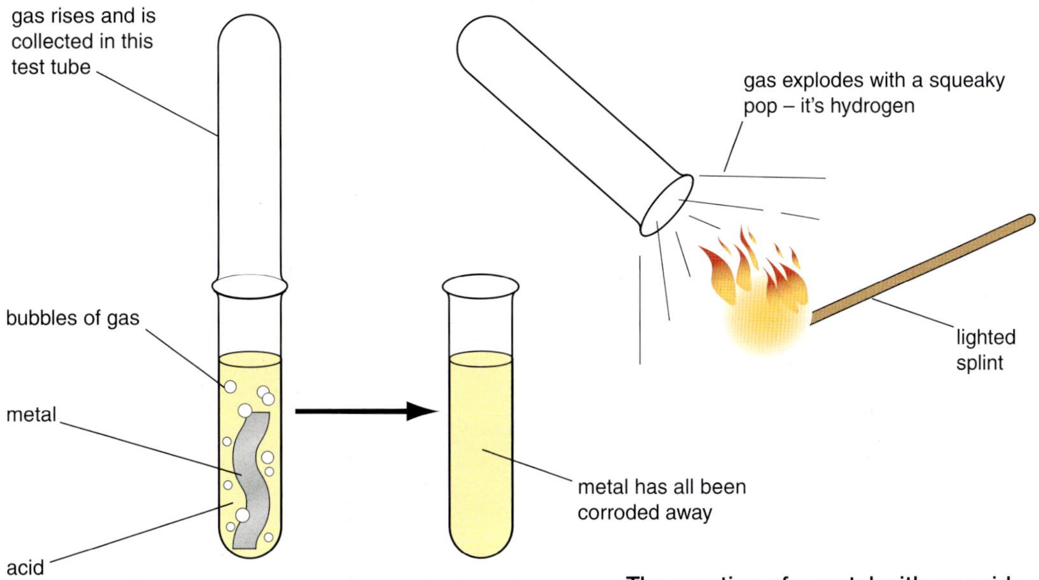

The reaction of a metal with an acid

The bubbles are caused by a gas being produced. If we collect this gas and put a lighted splint to it, the gas explodes with a squeak. This tells us that the gas is hydrogen. Putting a lighted splint to a gas is the test for hydrogen.

Acids also corrode substances called **carbonates**. Limestone is a carbonate. When an acid is added to limestone it fizzes. If we collect the gas and then mix the gas with limewater, the limewater goes milky. This tells us that the gas is carbon dioxide. Mixing a gas with limewater is the test for carbon dioxide.

Saying things out loud can help things stick in your brain. Try repeating: 'Acid plus metal produces hydrogen' and 'Acid plus carbonate produces carbon dioxide'.

4 Name one product when hydrochloric acid reacts with magnesium metal.

5 Name one product when sulfuric acid reacts with limestone.

6 a What is the test for hydrogen?

b What is the test for carbon dioxide?

7 An acid is added to limestone and bubbles of gas are collected. A lighted splint is put to the gas. What do you think happens?

FACT Fossil hunters get fossils out of limestone by corroding the limestone away with acid.

How did I do?

	✔
I know what a chemical reaction is.	☐
I know how acids react with metals.	☐
I know how acids react with carbonates.	☐

12: Burning

In this unit you will learn to answer these questions:

- What new substances are made when materials burn in air or oxygen?
- What is produced when fuels burn?
- What is needed for things to burn?

Get started

Burning wood is a chemical reaction. Draw a diagram of this chemical reaction. Label your diagram to show how you know it's a chemical reaction.

FACT Metals like aluminium, iron, magnesium and titanium are ground into fine powders to be combusted in fireworks.

Some metals burn when they are heated in air. For example magnesium burns with a bright white flame.

Burning (properly called **combustion**) is a chemical reaction. In the case of magnesium one of the reactants is magnesium and the other is oxygen from the air. The product is an oxide called magnesium oxide.

We can show this as a **word equation**:

magnesium + oxygen ⟶ magnesium oxide

For combustion to occur you need heat, a **fuel** and oxygen. The air contains 20% oxygen. Things burn much better in 100% oxygen.

Remember the three things needed for combustion using the 'fire triangle' shown here.

Practice

1. How can you tell that burning magnesium is a chemical reaction?
2. The flame from burning magnesium is brighter in pure oxygen. Why?
3. Calcium will also burn in air. Write a word equation for this reaction.

A fuel is something that contains a store of energy that can be turned into heat energy, usually by burning.

Wood, candle wax, natural gas, coal, petrol and oil are all fuels. These fuels all contain carbon, so when they combust carbon dioxide is produced.

They also all contain hydrogen, so when they combust hydrogen oxide (more commonly called water!) is produced.

The general word equation looks like this:

$$\text{fuel} + \text{oxygen} \longrightarrow \text{carbon dioxide} + \text{water}$$

Natural gas is mainly methane. The word equation for burning natural gas is:

$$\text{methane} + \text{oxygen} \longrightarrow \text{carbon dioxide} + \text{water}$$

In an experiment, a candle was placed in a trough of water and lit. Then a jar was placed over it. The water rose inside the jar and the candle went out.

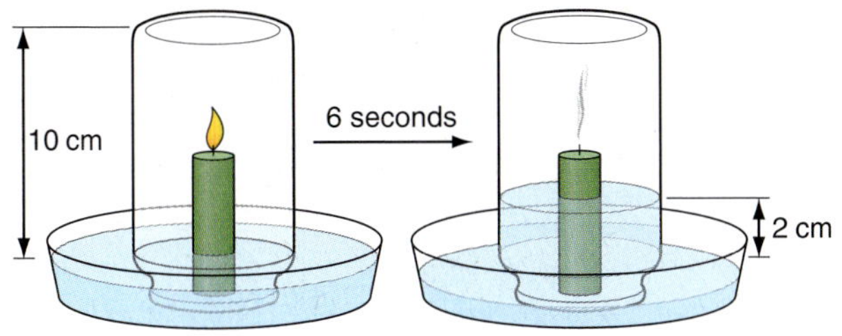

The candle went out because it had run out of oxygen. To put out a fire you need to take away the oxygen (air) or the fuel or the heat.

4 What is a fuel?

5 Candle wax is made of carbon and hydrogen. Write out a word equation for the combustion of candle wax.

6 a In the above experiment, why did the candle go out?

b Explain why the water rose 2 cm up the jar.

7 Why will water put out a bonfire?

8 Write a word equation for the combustion of hydrogen.

FACT Spontaneous human combustion is when a human body catches fire but nothing around it burns. No one knows the cause.

Use the 'fire triangle' (shown on the opposite page) to remember how to put out a fire. You need to remove one side of the triangle.

How did I do?

	✔
I know what new substances are made when materials burn in air or oxygen.	☐
I know what is produced when fuels burn.	☐
I know what is needed for things to burn.	☐

13: Solids, liquids and gases

In this unit you will learn to answer these questions:

- How can we explain evidence from experiments?
- How are theories created?
- What are the differences between solids, liquids and gases?

Get started

Sort these substances into three groups: solids, liquids, gases.

air carbon dioxide hydrogen milk sand stone water wood

FACT There's only one substance that exists naturally in all three states – water.

There are three forms that a substance can take. It can be a **solid**, a **liquid** or a **gas**. These are the three **states of matter**.

Solids (for example a brick) have these properties:

- They don't flow easily.
- They keep their shapes.
- They keep their **volumes**.
- They cannot be squashed.

Liquids (for example orange juice) have these properties:

- They flow easily.
- They take up the shapes of their containers.
- They keep their volumes.
- They cannot be squashed.

Do you find it easier to remember facts as lists with headings and bullet points or as a table? Draw out a table of the properties of solids, liquids and gases and find out!

Gases (for example air) have these properties:

- They flow easily.
- They take up the shapes of their containers.
- They expand to fill their containers.
- They can be squashed.

Practice

1 Which states of matter:

a keep their volumes

b keep their shapes

c can be squashed?

Scientists try to explain why things are like they are. They ask questions like: 'Why can't liquids be squashed?' and 'Why don't solids flow?'.

Scientists make **observations** or do experiments to collect **data**. They then try to think up ideas to explain their observations and data. A good idea can explain lots of things and can be used to say what will happen in future experiments – it can be used to make **predictions**.

An idea that has successfully been used to make predictions that have been right is called a **theory**. Over time, theories often change and sometimes they are found not to be correct after all.

The theory that explains why the states of matter have their properties is called the **particle theory**. It says that everything is made of tiny little particles that you can't see.

FACT

There have been many theories that have been disproved over the years, including ones like the Earth being flat and the Moon being made of carbon.

2 What is a theory?

3 What is a prediction?

4 A certain substance can flow. What could it be?

5 What does the particle theory say that iron is made of?

6 Anil says, 'Water should be the only liquid.' If this were true, think up one way in which this would be a good thing and one way in which this would be a bad thing. Then find out an interesting fact about water.

How did I do?

	✔
I know how we can explain evidence from experiments.	☐
I know how theories are created.	☐
I know what the differences are between solids, liquids and gases.	☐

14: The particle theory

In this unit you will learn to answer these questions:

- How can the particle model explain the differences between solids, liquids and gases?
- How can the particle model explain other phenomena?

Get started

Imagine that you could look down a hugely powerful microscope and see particles. Draw what you think iron would look like.

There are two important points to remember about the particle theory:

- Particles are arranged differently in different states.
- Particles are always moving.

FACT There is a theory that if you get a substance cold enough its particles will stop moving. This temperature is −273.15 °C, but so far scientists have not been able to make anything this cold.

Particles in a solid are in a regular framework. They are held together by strong **bonds** and only jiggle about fixed positions. A solid cannot flow because the particles can't move past each other. A solid cannot be squashed because the particles can't get any closer to each other.

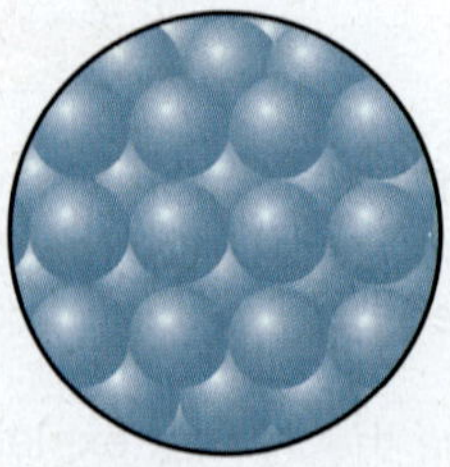

Particles in a solid

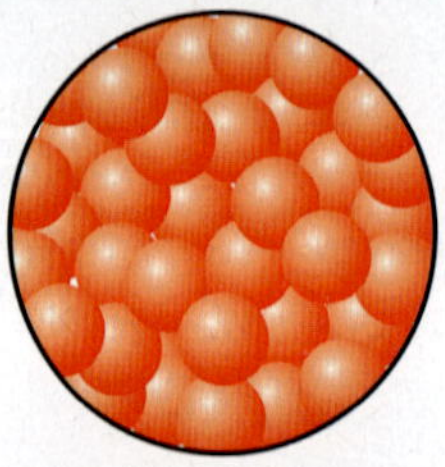

Particles in a liquid

Particles in a liquid are arranged randomly. They are held together by bonds that allow the particles to move past each other. This is why liquids flow. A liquid can't be squashed because the particles can't get any closer together.

Particles in a gas are not held together. They are whizzing around all over the place and that's why gases fill a container they're put into. A gas can be squashed because the particles can get closer together.

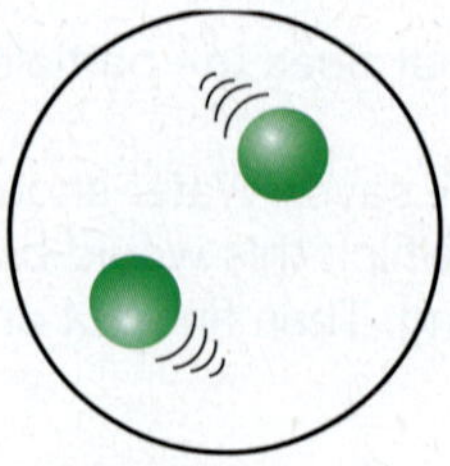

Particles in a gas

Practice

1. Draw diagrams of the particles in:

   a magnesium

   b helium

   c mercury.

The particle theory can be used to explain **diffusion**, **dissolving** and the **pressure** of gases.

Diffusion is when particles spread through another liquid or gas. You can smell if someone is wearing perfume or aftershave because particles of the perfume spread through the air and reach your nose. The air does not need to be mixed for this to happen since gas particles are always whizzing around.

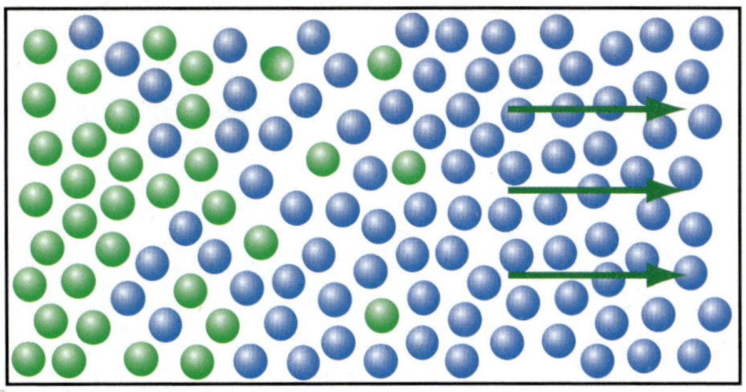

Particles of one gas (green) diffusing through another gas (blue)

If you drop instant-coffee granules into a glass of cold water, you will see a brown colour spread through the water. The coffee particles are diffusing through the water.

Eventually you can't see the coffee granules any longer because they have dissolved. Dissolving is when the particles of a solid have all separated from each other and spread throughout a liquid.

Gas particles hit the walls of the container they are in. The constant hitting of particles against the walls produces a pressure, which pushes out on the walls of the container. If you make the container smaller, but don't let any gas out, the particles hit the walls more often and the pressure increases.

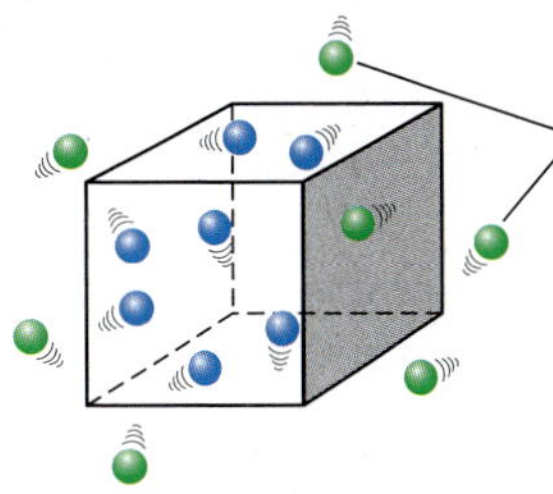

Gases produce a pressure on their container

2 You have been asked to write two definitions for a dictionary. Write down how you would define:

a diffusion

b dissolving.

3 A sugar lump disappears if it is dropped into hot water. Why?

4 If you suck all the air out of a tin, the tin crumples. Why?

5 Copy this diagram and add labels to explain how a drinking straw works.

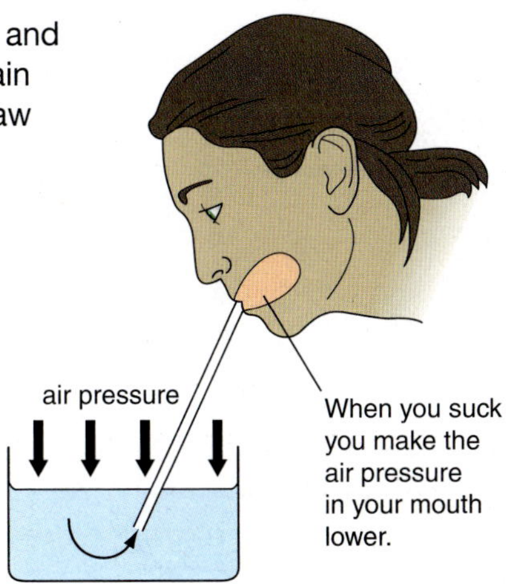

FACT

All the air around you creates a pressure that pushes on you but you're used to it and don't feel it. Our bodies are designed to work with this pressure. Astronauts must wear pressurised space suits, or else they would die.

How did I do?

I know how the particle model can explain the differences between solids, liquids and gases. ✔ ☐

I know how the particle model can explain other phenomena. ☐

15: Solutions

In this unit you will learn to answer these questions:

- How can we tell whether a liquid is a mixture?
- How much salt can we get from rock salt?
- What happens to the solute when a solution is made?
- How can we separate solvents from solutes?

Get started

Which is the odd one out and why?

brick   cement   salt   sand   steel   stone

When a substance **dissolves** we often can't see it any longer, but it's still there; it's just that its particles have separated and spread out. Solids that dissolve are said to be **soluble**. Solids that don't dissolve are **insoluble**.

FACT The UK has about 140 miles of tunnels that are used to mine about 2 million tonnes of rock salt each year.

Seawater contains salt dissolved in water. It is a **mixture** of more than one substance. You can't see the salt in seawater, but you know it's there because it tastes salty. If you let some seawater dry out, the water turns to gas and leaves behind the salt.

Rock salt is a mixture of salt and rock. To make pure salt you stir crushed rock salt with water. The salt dissolves but the rock doesn't. You then **filter** the mixture to remove the insoluble rock, and then evaporate the water to leave behind the salt.

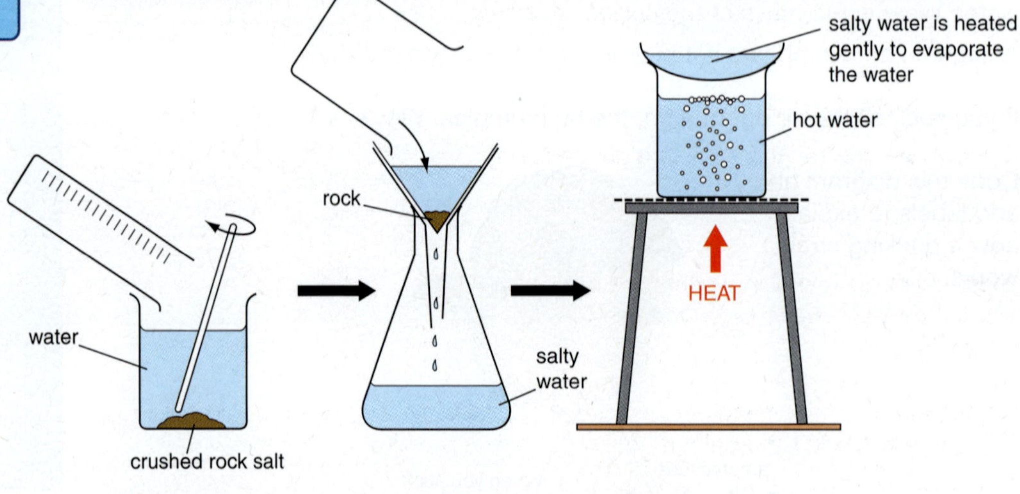

Getting pure salt from rock salt

Practice

1. What is a mixture?
2. Which of these are soluble?

   plastic   salt   sand   stone   sugar   wood

3. Some rock salt had a mass of 100 g. The salt obtained from it had a mass of 40 g. Why did the salt have less mass than the rock salt?

When you dissolve a solid in a liquid you get a **solution**. A solution is always see-through. If you mix an insoluble solid in a liquid you often get a **suspension** (e.g. muddy water). Suspensions are not see-through.

Salty water is a solution of salt and water. The substance that has dissolved is the **solute** and the liquid is the **solvent**. The mass of a solution is the same as the mass of the solvent plus the mass of the solute. No matter is lost during dissolving.

Remember that only solVents eVaporate. Solutes don't and they get left behind. That's why rain isn't salty!

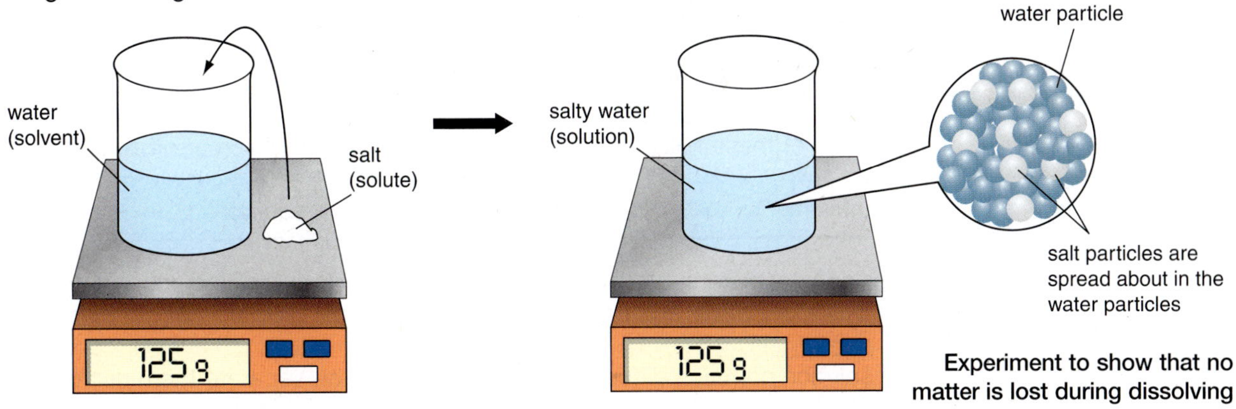

Experiment to show that no matter is lost during dissolving

You can separate the solute from the solution by **evaporation**. If you **condense** the evaporated water back to a liquid you can collect the pure solvent. Evaporation (turning a liquid into a gas) followed by **condensation** (turning a gas into a liquid) is called **distillation**. The diagram shows some simple distillation apparatus.

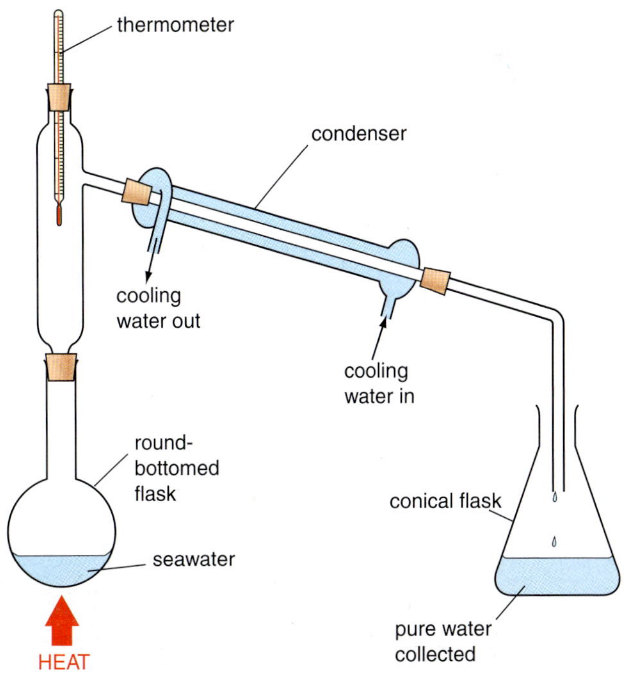

Simple distillation apparatus

4 70 g of copper sulphate is added to 250 g of water. What is the mass of the copper sulphate solution that is formed?

5 a What is a solution?

b How can you tell that milk is a suspension?

c Apart from milk, name a liquid mixture which is not a solution.

6 Gloss paint dissolves in white spirit but not in water. Write out these sentences and fill in the gaps.

Gloss paint is _____ in water but it is _____ in white spirit. When it forms a _____ in white spirit the paint is the _____ and the white spirit is the _____.

7 What is the opposite of evaporation?

FACT Dry cleaning uses a solvent other than water to get clothes clean. Early dry cleaners used petrol as the solvent!

How did I do?

	✔
I know how we can tell whether a liquid is a mixture.	☐
I know how much salt we can get from rock salt.	☐
I know what happens to the solute when a solution is made.	☐
I know how we can separate solvents from solutes.	☐

16: More about dissolving

In this unit you will learn to answer these questions:

- How can chromatography separate and identify substances in mixtures?
- Is there a limit to the amount of solid that will dissolve in a liquid?

Get started

Which of these liquids are one pure substance and which are mixtures?

black ink | cranberry juice | orange squash | water

In science, a **pure** substance contains only one thing. Distilled water is pure but tap water, seawater and mineral water are mixtures; they are not pure water.

If a solution contains different solutes you can often separate them using **chromatography**. The diagram shows a **chromatogram** made by doing chromatography on four different inks.

Labelled diagrams are a good way to learn things. Draw a labelled diagram to summarise the information on this page.

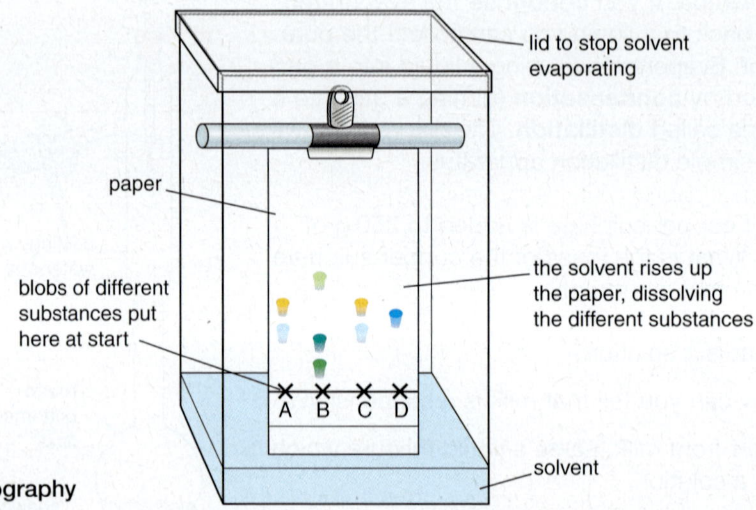

Chromatography

Different solutes have different particle sizes. Larger particles travel more slowly than smaller ones and so the solutes are separated. Blobs of the same colour that reach the same height on the chromatogram are the same substance.

Solutes in urine are separated using chromatography in hospitals. Stains are used to make the solutes show up.

FACT The Food Standards Agency uses chromatography to check that foods don't contain things that they shouldn't.

Practice

1. What is a pure substance?
2. Look at the chromatogram.
   a Is ink B a pure substance?
   b How do you know?
   c Which ink contains only one dye?
   d Which two inks are the same?
3. Why would a hospital want to find out what was in someone's urine?

When you add sugar to hot tea it dissolves, but there is a maximum amount of sugar you can add. When no more of a solute will dissolve in a solvent you have a **saturated solution**.

The amount of a solute that will dissolve in a certain amount of solvent is its **solubility**. The table on the right shows how much of various solutes will dissolve in 100 cm^3 of water at 25 °C. Different solutes have different solubilities.

Substance	Solubility at 25 °C (g /100 cm^3 of water)
aspirin	0.33
sodium hydroxide	42
sugar	211
salt (sodium chloride)	35.7

Generally, you can increase a substance's solubility by increasing the temperature. The graph shows how the solubility of sugar increases with temperature.

Graph to show how the solubility of sugar increases with temperature

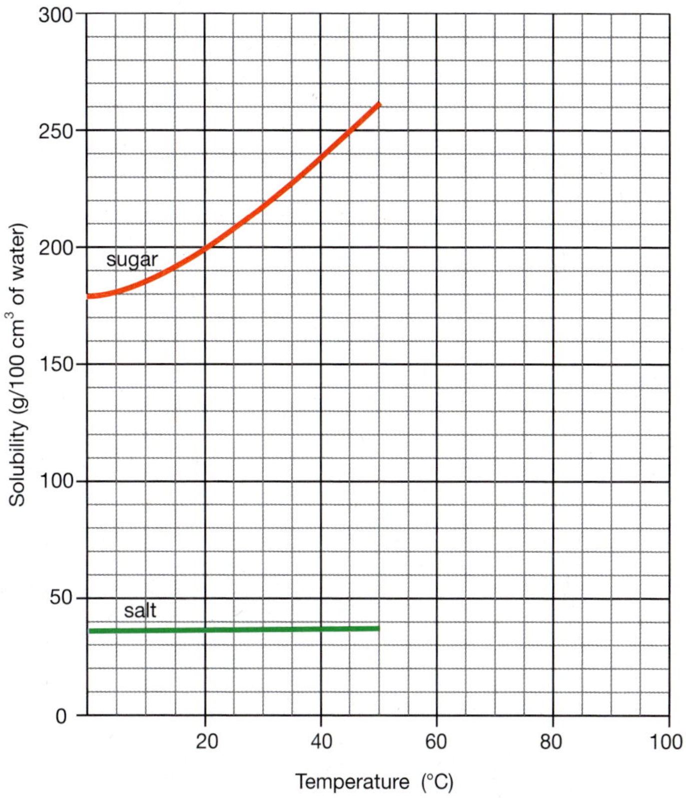

4 a What is a saturated solution?

b How could you make a saturated solution of sugar in water?

5 Look at the table above. Which substance is:

a the most soluble

b the least soluble?

6 Look at the graph.

a What happens to the solubility of sugar as the temperature increases?

b What is the solubility of sugar at 0 °C?

c What do you think the solubility of salt will be at 100 °C?

7 Why does sugar dissolve better in hot tea than in cold water?

8 A saturated solution of benzoic acid has been made in hot water. As the water cools, crystals of benzoic acid are seen to form. Why is this?

FACT Gases also dissolve in liquids but they get less soluble as temperature increases. Fish in streams and ponds often die in very hot weather because there is too little oxygen in the water.

How did I do?

I know how chromatography can separate and identify substances in mixtures.	☐ ✔
I know there is a limit to the amount of solid that will dissolve in a liquid.	☐

17: Fuels

In this unit you will learn to answer these questions:

- Why are fuels useful?
- What are fossil fuels?

Get started

Unmuddle these words and phrases to make the names of four fuels.

COLA OR PELT SULTANA RAG SEE LID

Fuels are substances that can be used to release heat energy. When they are burned, they also release light energy. Light, heat and movement are all different types of energy.

Natural gas is the fuel that is burned in a **Bunsen burner**. As the gas burns it gives out light energy and heat energy.

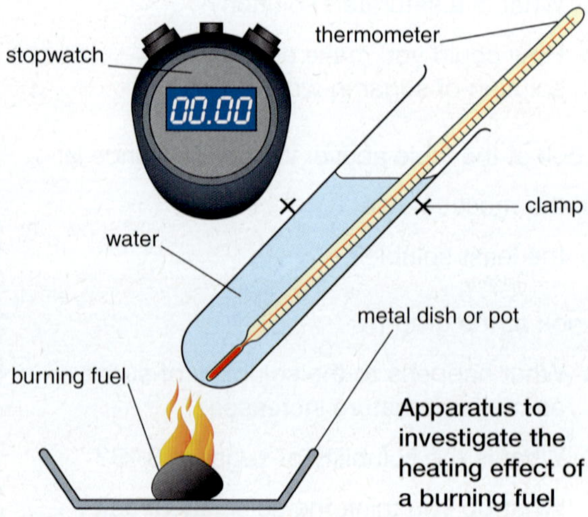

Apparatus to investigate the heating effect of a burning fuel

Different fuels give out different amounts of heat energy. In an investigation a fuel is burned and the temperature of a volume of water is measured after 5 minutes.

Fuel	Temperature of water at start (°C)	Temperature of water after 5 minutes (°C)
paraffin	24	44
ethanol	24	43
wood	25	37
firelighter	25	69

For a **fair test** we must only change the fuel in each measurement and keep everything else the same (e.g. the amount of water).

We should repeat the measurements for each fuel, to check them.

FACT 'Burning off calories' means using up the energy from food that's stored in your body. Nothing actually burns, although heat energy is released.

Practice

1 What energies are released by burning natural gas?

2 Name as many things as you can that need to be kept the same to make the investigation above a fair test.

3 a Copy the table above and add another column titled 'Temperature rise (°C)'.

b What was the best fuel?

c How do you know it was the best?

Some fuels are called **fossil fuels** because they are made from the remains of prehistoric animals and plants. Examples include **peat**, **natural gas**, **coal** and **oil** (and all the fuels made from oil, like petrol and diesel).

Fossil fuels form when organisms die and are crushed by layers of rock forming above them. This process takes millions of years.

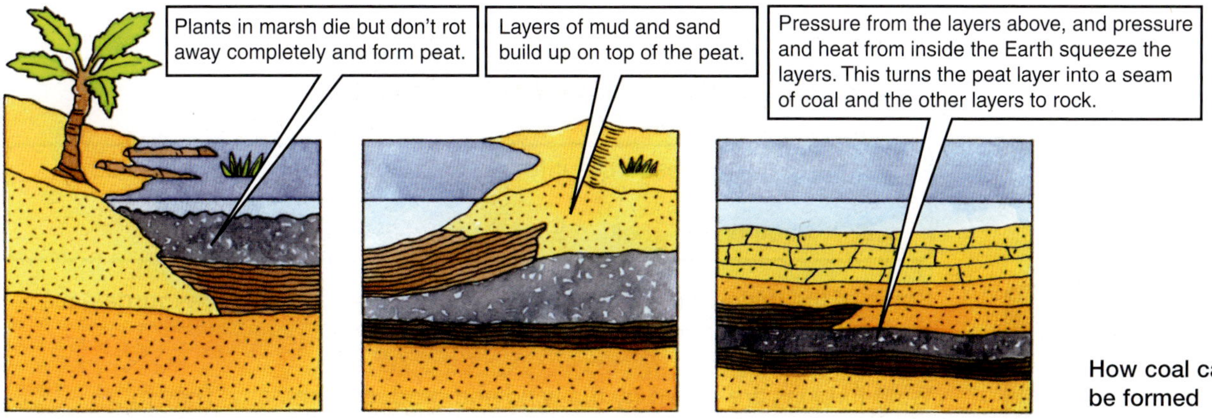

How coal can be formed

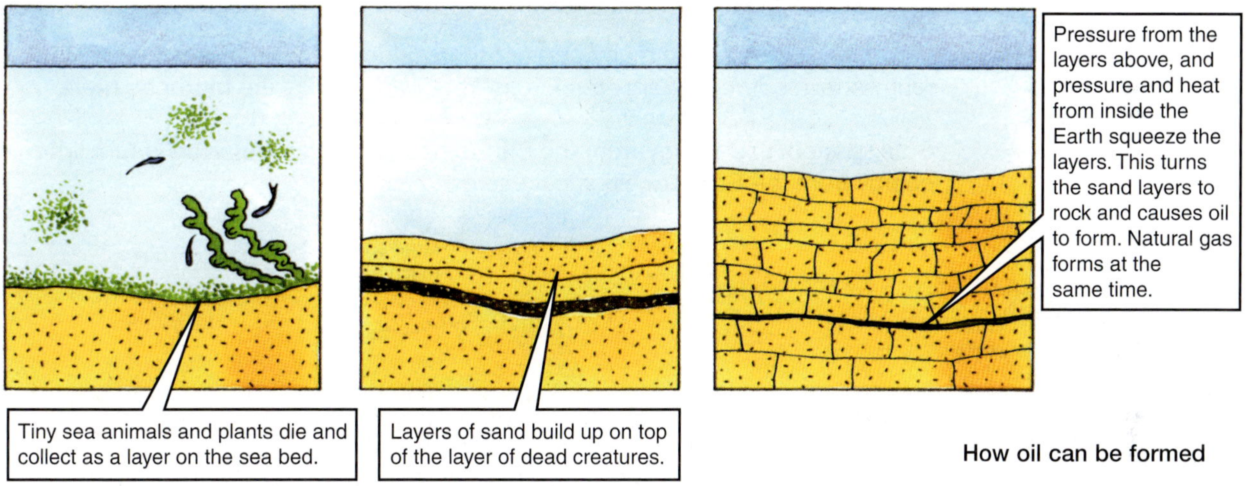

How oil can be formed

Once fossil fuels have been used they are gone forever and cannot be remade. Fuels like this are called **non-renewable** fuels. Fossil fuels are running out so we must use them carefully and not waste the energy that they provide us with. Ways to save energy include using cars less and making sure electrical devices are switched off when we're not using them.

4 What is a fossil fuel?

5 Write a list of three short bullet points to explain how coal is formed.

6 What is oil formed from?

7 Why is natural gas non-renewable?

8 Design a poster to show ways in which your family could save energy.

Writing summaries is a useful way of learning. Write a summary of the information on these two pages using up to 60 words! Write your summary on a card and keep it. Come back to it at a later date.

FACT A seam of coal inside Burning Mountain in Australia has been burning for 6000 years.

How did I do?

	✔
I know why fuels are useful.	☐
I know what fossil fuels are.	☐

18: Energy resources

In this unit you will learn to answer these questions:

- What are renewable energy resources?
- How do living things use energy?

Get started

Sort these energy resources into two groups. Give each group a title.

coal geothermal oil Sun water wind wood

FACT Back in 1908, Henry Ford designed his first Model T cars to run on ethanol made from wheat. Ethanol is a biomass fuel.

Some of the things we use to provide us with energy (**energy resources**) are **renewable**, which means that they will not run out.

Wind turbines are driven by the wind and produce electricity. They turn movement energy of the wind into electrical energy. Wind doesn't run out!

Wood is used as fuel in many parts of the world. It can be re-grown so it is a renewable resource. Energy resources from living things are **biomass fuels**.

Solar panels use energy from the Sun to heat up water. **Solar cells** turn light energy from the Sun into electrical energy.

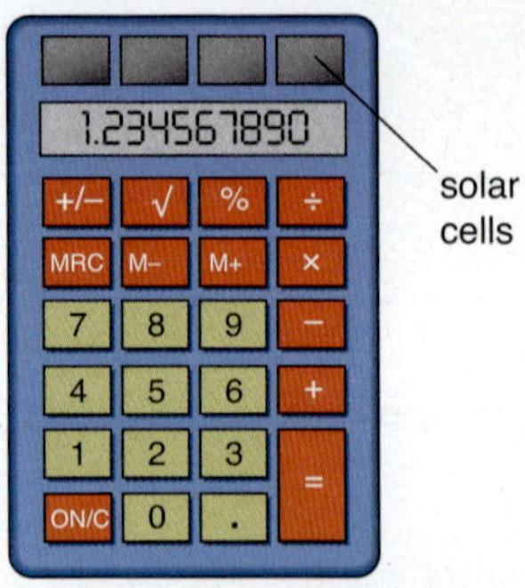

Solar cells in a calculator

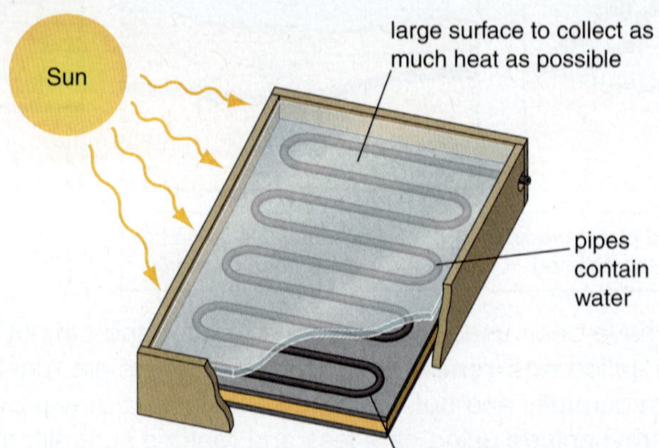

Solar panel

Think up a mnemonic for the different renewable energy resources.

Heat from rocks deep underground can be used to heat water and make electricity. This is **geothermal power**.

The power of water held back by a dam can be used to turn **turbines**, which produce electricity. This is **hydroelectric power**.

Practice

1. What is a biomass fuel?
2. Why won't solar cells make electricity 24 hours a day?
3. Design a way to provide electricity for a town in the year 2050.

All living things need energy. Plants get their energy from the Sun. Animals get their energy from food.

Foods have **nutrition information** labels on them that tell us what is in them. These labels show how much 'energy' is in the food.

Nutrition Information	Per 40g serving	Per 100g
Energy	506kJ (121kcal)	1265kJ (302kcal)
Protein	4.7g	11.8g
Carbohydrate	20.9g	52.3g
Fat	1.9g	4.7g
Fibre	9.9g	24.8g
Sodium	0.2g	0.5g

Energy is measured in **joules** (**J**). One joule is about the amount of energy needed to raise a medium-sized apple by 1 metre. One **kilojoule** is 1000 joules. Calories are the old-fashioned units for energy.

The energy stored in food is called **chemical energy**. Your body turns this into other sorts of energy (e.g. **heat energy**, **movement energy**). You use more chemical energy when you exercise. The apparatus shown on page 40 is used to find out how much energy is in dry food.

Plants make their own food. They turn **light energy** from the Sun into chemical energy, which is stored in substances like starch. We get this chemical energy when we eat the plants!

4 Where do you get your energy from?

5 Look at the nutrition label above.

a How much energy is in 100 g of this food?

b How many apples could you raise by 1 m if you ate 40 g of the food?

6 Draw a flow diagram, like the one above, to show how you get energy to ride a bike from eating potatoes.

7 How could you find out which of two breakfast cereals contained more energy, without looking at the boxes?

FACT

Fireflies produce light energy using the chemical energy in their food.

How did I do?

	✔
I know what renewable energy resources are.	☐
I know how living things use energy.	☐

19: Electrical circuits

In this unit you will learn to answer these questions:

- How do electrical circuits work?
- What happens in a circuit?

Get started

Draw a diagram showing an electrical cell connected to a bulb, so that the bulb lights.

FACT Electricity travels around a circuit at 300 000 km/s (over 1 *billion* kilometres per hour).

A **bulb** turns **electrical energy** into **light energy** when it's connected to a cell to make a circuit. The electricity that carries the electrical energy flows from the cell, through metal things and back to the cell. Electricity won't flow if there are gaps. A circuit with no gaps is a **complete circuit**. A **switch** can make or close a gap in a circuit to turn **components** on and off.

We use circuit diagrams to show circuits, with **symbols** for the components.

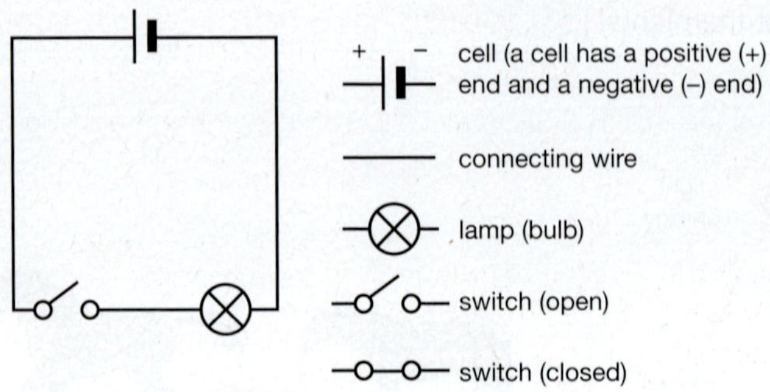

Invent silly ways to remember which way round things go. For example, the longer line of the cell symbol is '+' because a '+' sign has a longer total length of line in it than a '–' sign!

If more than one bulb is connected to a cell, both bulbs will be less bright. Bulbs connected one after the other are said to be connected **in series**.

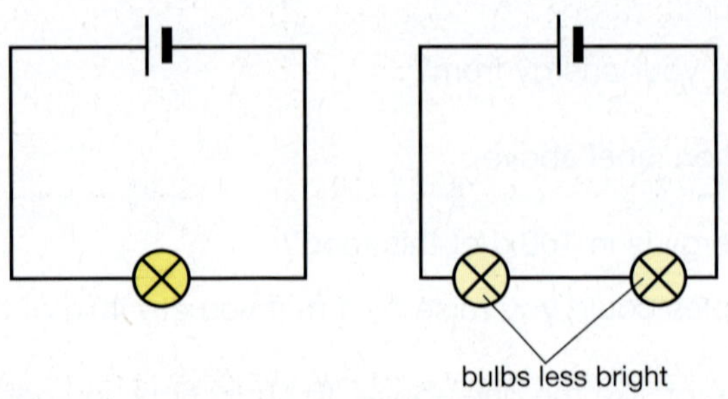

Practice

1. Name one component of a circuit.
2. Why won't the bulb in the top diagram light up?
3. a Draw a diagram of a circuit with three bulbs in series and one cell.
   b How bright will these bulbs be compared with a circuit with two bulbs and one cell?

Flowing electricity is called a **current**. A current is measured by connecting an **ammeter** in series with other components.

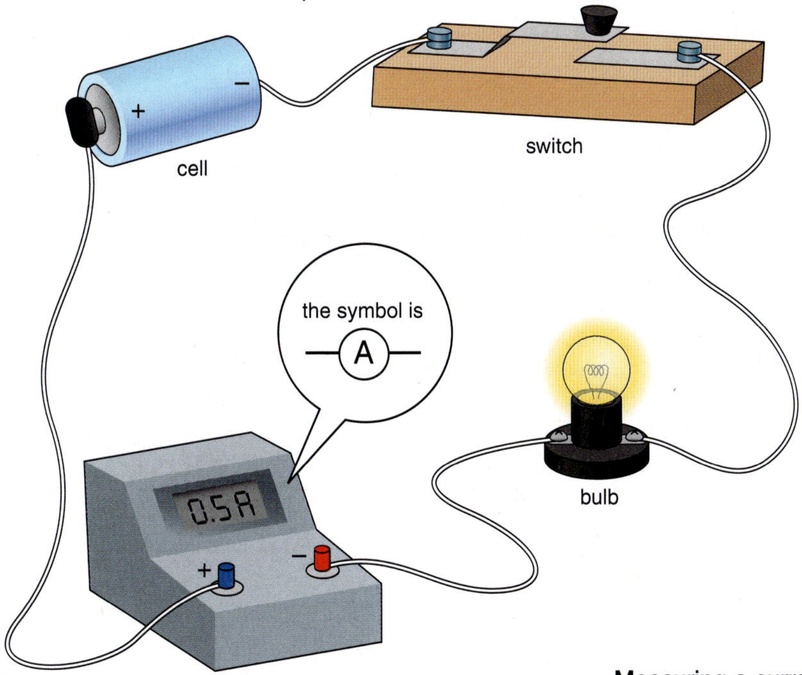

Measuring a current

Ammeters measure current in **amps** (**A**). The current is the same all the way around a circuit – it does *not* get used up.

Bulbs create **resistance** in a circuit. Resistance slows the current down and so the more bulbs, the less the current in the whole circuit. The slower the current, the less bright the bulbs. Components called resistors can also reduce the current in a circuit.

A current is caused by a cell. The more **voltage** a cell has, the greater its 'pushing power' and the faster a current will flow. Voltage is measured in **volts** (**V**).

Lots of cells connected together make a **battery**. The drawings below show three batteries (the dotted line means 'lots of cells').

4 Draw a circuit diagram for the circuit at the top of the page.

5 Three cells have voltages 1.5 V, 6 V and 9 V. Which will produce the biggest current in a circuit?

6 Look at the symbols shown above for the batteries X, Y and Z.

a Make up a rule for how cells should be connected to make a battery.

b How many cells are there in batteries X, Y and Z?

How did I do?

✔

I know how electrical circuits work. ☐

I know what happens in a circuit. ☐

Use a **model** to think about things that you can't see. To think about electricity, imagine a river of hot water. The heat is like the electrical energy. The flow of water is like the current. The water carries the heat, which is lost as the water cools. The water itself is not used up and so the current doesn't get used up. An electrical current loses the electrical energy it's carrying to bulbs in a circuit, but this does not slow it down. However, this model can't be used to think about resistance. A better model (using a central heating system) is in the next unit.

FACT

Amps and volts are named after famous scientists who studied electricity – André Marie Ampère (1775–1836) and Alessandro Volta (1745–1827)

20: More circuits

In this unit you will learn to answer these questions:
- How can we explain what happens in electrical circuits?
- What kinds of circuits are useful and what are the hazards?

Get started

This is a central heating system. It can be used as a model (see page 45) for an electrical circuit. Draw out the electrical circuit for which it's a model.

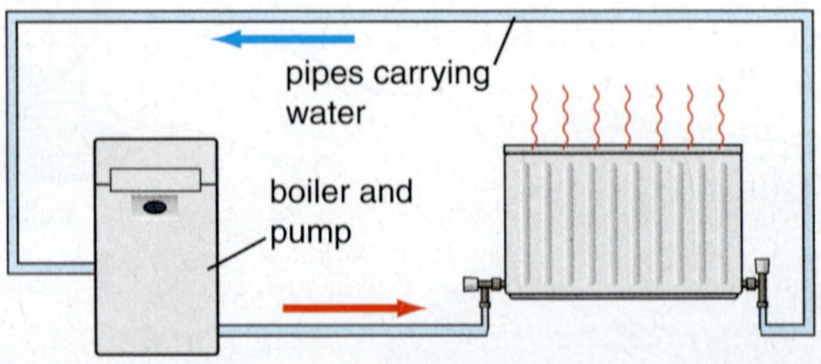

The model above can be used to think about current (water flow in pipes), a cell (the boiler), electrical energy (heat) and a bulb (the radiator).

It can also be used to think about resistance. The radiator pipes are thinner than the other pipes. This makes it difficult for water to flow through them and so the speed of the water through the whole system is slowed. It's more difficult for current to flow through circuits containing resistors and bulbs.

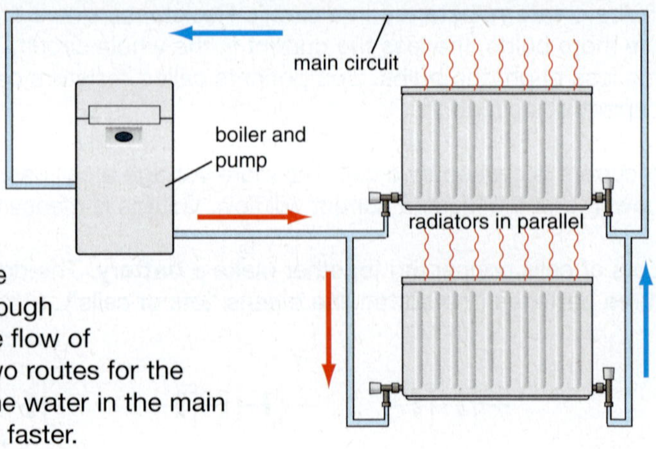

Another radiator can be added **in parallel**. Although each radiator slows the flow of water, there are now two routes for the water to take and so the water in the main part of the circuit flows faster.

In an electrical parallel circuit, the current in the main circuit is equal to the sum of all the currents in the branches. Two bulbs in parallel shine as brightly as one bulb on its own since the extra branch allows more current to flow.

FACT

A current is caused by flowing tiny particles called electrons. Scientists aren't sure how big they are but they're something like 0.000 000 00 0 000 03 mm wide.

Practice

1. Copy the paragraph above starting 'Another radiator...' and change the words so that it's now about an electrical circuit. Draw a parallel circuit with a cell and two bulbs.
2. A parallel circuit has two branches, each with one bulb. A current of 0.5 A flows through each branch. How much current flows in the main circuit?
3. How is the central heating system not a good model? Think about breaking a water pipe and breaking a wire.

House lights are connected in parallel. Christmas tree lights are often connected in series, which is cheaper. However, if one bulb blows, the circuit is broken and all the bulbs go out.

Resistors are used to control the current in circuits in electrical devices. A variable resistor can change the amount of current in a circuit. Variable resistors are used in dimmer switches.

Sometimes things go wrong in a circuit and too much current flows through a device, causing a fire. That's why plugs have **fuses** fitted. Too high a current heats the wire in the fuse until it melts, breaking the circuit.

We use **mains electricity** at 230 V in our homes, which gives you an **electric shock** if you touch it. Higher voltages can cause burns and even death. Your body contains nerves, which normally carry tiny currents, but large voltages cause them to carry large currents that can stop them working. Nerves are important for controlling your heart and your breathing.

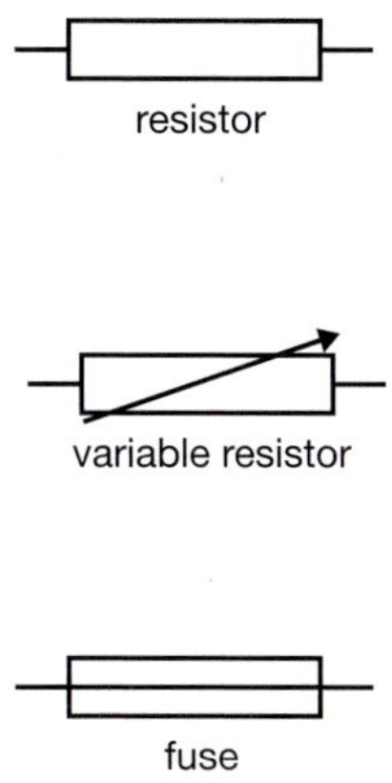

Symbols for more components

4 Why are house lights wired in parallel?

5 You have just built a four-roomed house and you need to plan the lighting. You need one bulb in each room. Each bulb must have a switch. Draw a circuit diagram to show the electrician how the lights should be wired up.

6 Why do electrical devices have fuses?

7 a One bulb in a circuit with one cell has 'normal brightness'. How bright are the bulbs in circuits X, Y and Z – dimmer than normal, normal or brighter?

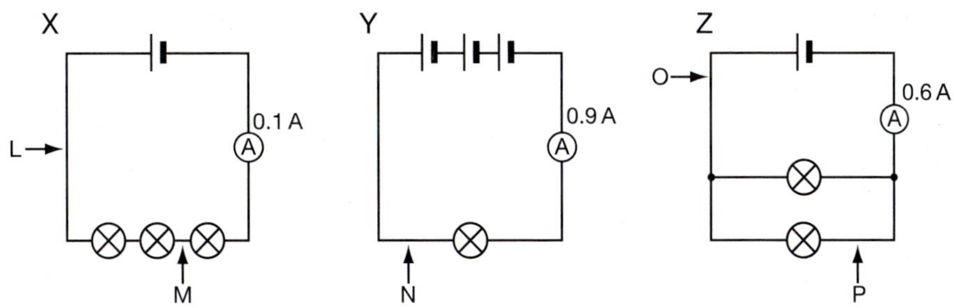

b The reading of an ammeter in each circuit is shown. What would the current be at points L, M, N, O and P in the circuits?

Fuses Fight Fires – again a memorable rhyme helps to remember things!

FACT About 100 people die every year by electrocution (killed by an electric current running through them).

How did I do?

I know how we can explain what happens in electrical circuits. ☐

I know what kinds of circuits are useful and what the hazards are. ☐

21: Different forces

In this unit you will learn to answer these questions:
- Where do we come across forces?
- Why do things float?
- How do different materials stretch?

Get started

Draw a diagram of yourself pushing a wheelbarrow and label the forces. (Think about the weight of the wheelbarrow, the strain force of your arms and your pushing force.)

Every force:
- is either a push or a pull
- has a certain size
- has a certain direction
- can change something's shape, and/or its speed, and/or its direction.

Contact forces need to touch things. **Friction** is a contact force that pulls back on things rubbing against each other. **Drag** is the friction caused by things moving through air or water (**air resistance** and **water resistance**). **Upthrust** pushes up on things that are in water. There are many other contact forces, like the force from your chair pushing up on you.

Non-contact forces include **static electricity**, **magnetism** and **gravity**.

A forcemeter is used to measure the force of gravity on something.

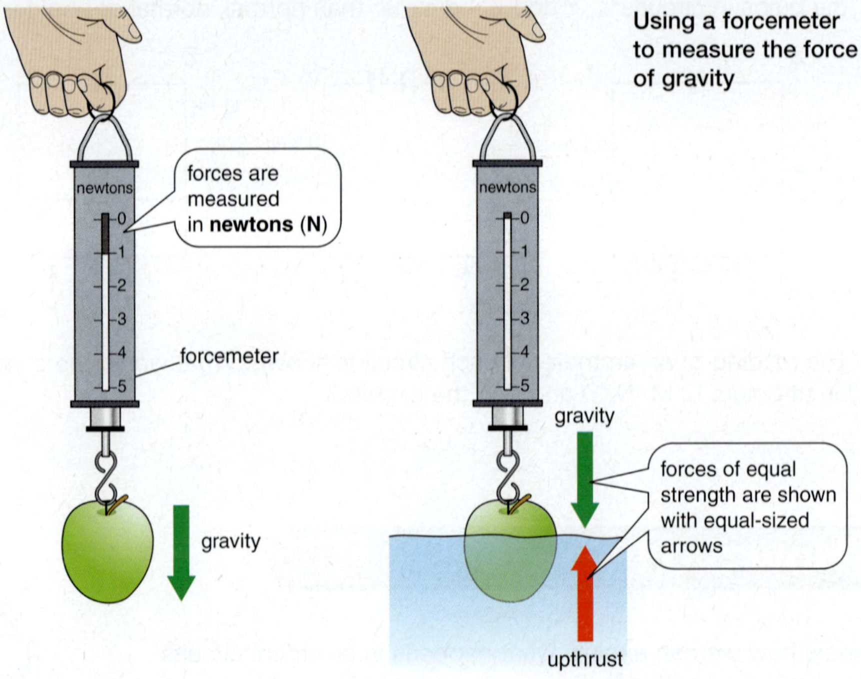

Using a forcemeter to measure the force of gravity

FACT The dimples on a golf ball are designed to reduce the effect of air resistance and so allow the ball to fly further through the air.

The force of gravity is lessened by forces like upthrust. When something floats the forces of gravity and upthrust are the same but in opposite directions – they are **balanced forces**.

Practice

1 a What is drag? b Name two types of drag.

2 a What is a non-contact force? b Name three non-contact forces.

Inside a forcemeter is a spring. When the apple is put on the forcemeter, the force of gravity causes the spring to stretch. After it has stretched a certain distance there is enough **strain force** in the spring to balance the force of gravity and so the spring stops getting longer.

In an investigation different weights were added to a spring and the amount that it stretched was measured. The graph below shows the results.

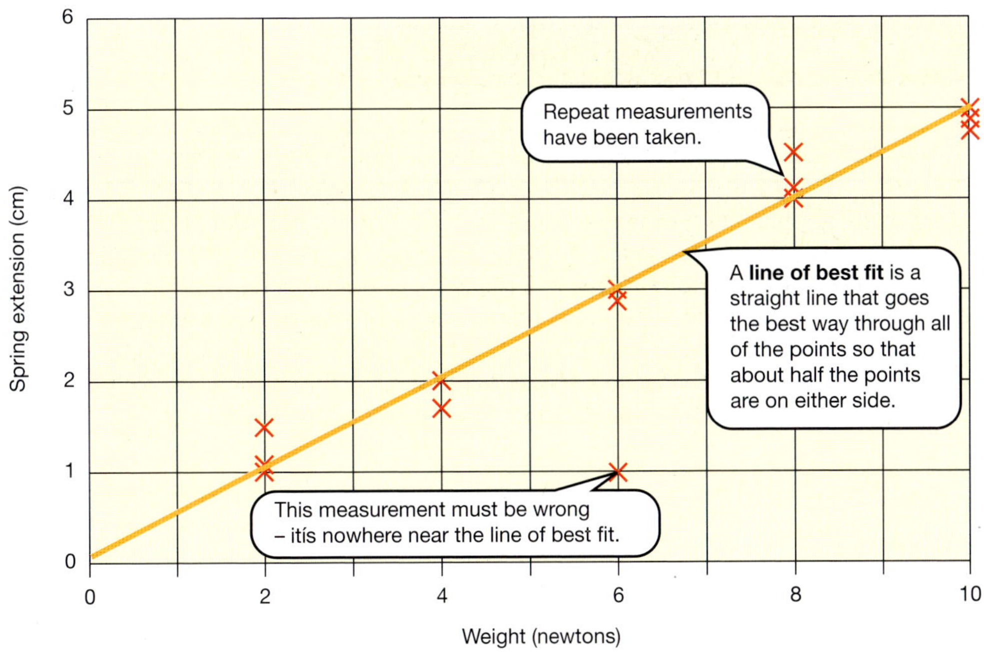

The **density** of a substance is how much mass a certain volume of that substance has. It's measured in units such as grams per centimetre cubed (g/cm^3). If substances have a lower density than water, then they float.

FACT

Gases also have a density. Helium balloons float because helium is less dense than air.

3 Copy the diagram of the forcemeter holding up the apple in the air. Add in another force arrow to show the force that balances the weight of the apple.

4 What are balanced forces?

5 Look at the graph above showing the spring extension for various weights.

a Why is it a good idea to take repeat measurements?

b What does the graph tell you? Try to come up with a rule for what happens when you add more weight to the spring.

Write the bold words on these two pages on pieces of paper and their meanings on other pieces. Then match the words with their meanings. Keep your pieces of paper to revise from.

How did I do?

	✔
I know where we come across forces.	☐
I know why things float.	☐
I know how different materials stretch.	☐

22: Weight and friction

In this unit you will learn to answer these questions:

- What is weight?
- What does friction do?
- What affects how quickly a car stops?

Get started

How much do you think a bag of six apples weighs? Have a guess.

A bag of six apples has a **mass** of about 600 g. It has a **weight** of about 6 newtons (6 N). Weight is the *force* with which gravity pulls on something and so it is measured in newtons. Mass is a measure of how much matter something contains. Every 1 kg mass has a weight of about 10 N on Earth.

When a wooden block is dragged across a surface, friction pulls back on the block. The amount of friction can be measured using a forcemeter.

Investigation to measure the amount of friction when pulling a wooden block

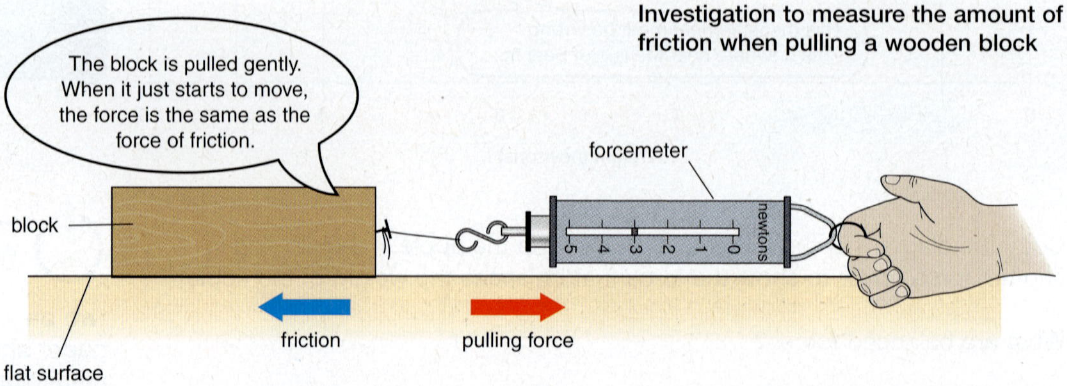

Write bulleted lists of ways to increase or decrease friction.

If more weight is added to the block the friction will be increased. The friction will also be increased by making the surface rougher or by increasing the area of the block in contact with the surface. Friction can be reduced by liquids (e.g. water, oil) between the surfaces. These liquids are called **lubricants**.

Practice

1. a A packet of sugar has a mass of 1 kg. What does it weigh?
   b A potato has a mass of 500 g. What does it weigh?
   c A melon weighs 20 N. What is its mass?
2. What is lubrication?
3. A wooden block was pulled across different surfaces. Rough sandpaper required 20 N of force to get the block to move, and fine sandpaper required 12 N of force.
   a What force do you predict would be needed for medium sandpaper?
   b What factors would need to be kept the same to make this a fair test?

FACT PTFE (Teflon®) produces the least friction. It is used in non-stick pans.

Friction can be a problem. The metal parts of an engine get hot and wear away because of friction. Oil is used as a lubricant to stop this happening. Fast cars have **streamlined** shapes so that air can flow across them easily, reducing air resistance.

However, friction is also useful in cars. Friction between the tyres and the road surface allows a car to move and stop without slipping and sliding. The brakes also use friction.

The diagram below shows the **stopping distances** of a car on a dry road. A stopping distance is made up of the **thinking distance** and the **braking distance**.

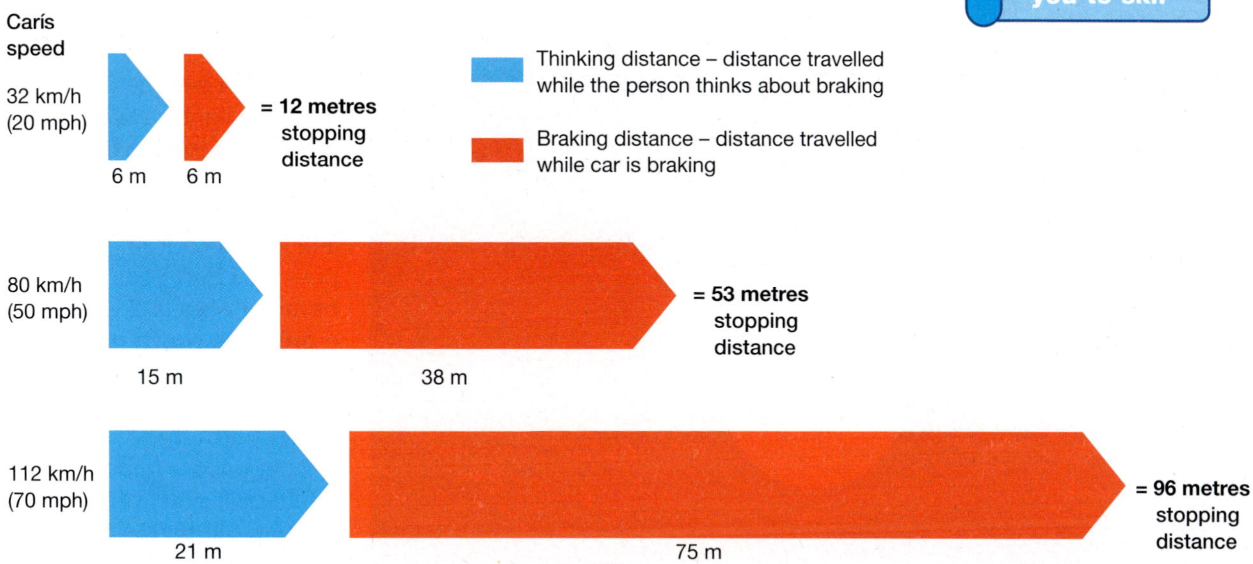

You can see from the diagram that the faster the speed, the longer it takes to stop. Cars take longer to stop in the rain because the water on the road acts as a lubricant.

4 a What is the stopping distance of a car going at 20 mph?

b What does ‘mph’ stand for?

5 Why should cars travel more slowly when it is raining?

6 Why do cars skid when they brake on ice?

7 Explain why friction is useful when you walk.

8 Think up one other way in which friction is useful and one other way in which it's not.

How did I do?

	✔
I know what weight is.	☐
I know what friction does.	☐
I know what affects how quickly a car stops.	☐

FACT

The friction caused by a moving ski on snow heats up the snow, causing it to melt. The thin layer of water produced acts as a lubricant and allows you to ski.

Have a go at drawing a concept map for the information on the last four pages. If you don't know what a concept map is, have a look at page 6. Use the diagram below to get started:

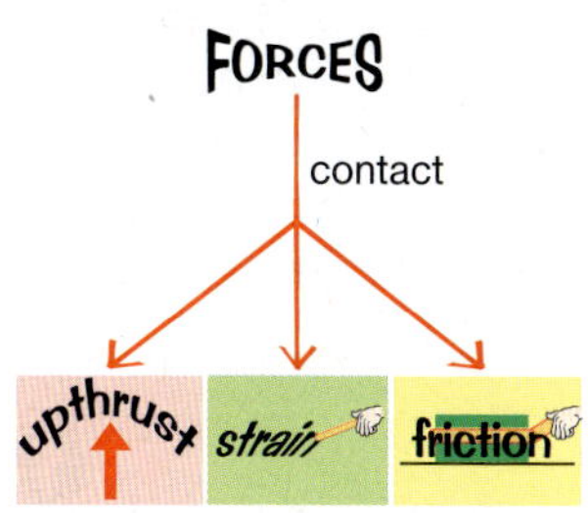

23: Sun, Moon and Earth

In this unit you will learn to answer these questions:

- Why do we have days, months and years?
- How do we see the Sun and Moon?

Get started

Why does the Moon shine? Draw a diagram for your answer.

Look at the letters on the diagram below and read the information about them.

The Earth's orbit

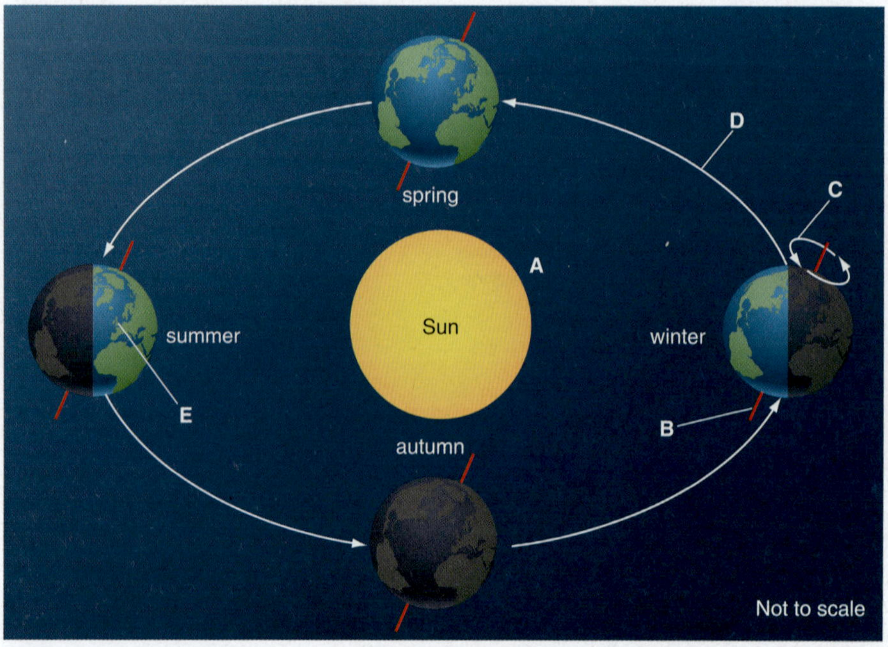

A You can see the Sun because light travels from the **Sun** to the **Earth**.

B The **axis** is an imaginary line that goes from pole to pole. The Earth has two **hemispheres** and each has a **pole** (the **North pole** and the **South pole**).

C The Earth takes 24 hours to spin once around its axis. As it spins parts of the Earth get lit by the Sun and then hidden from the Sun, giving **day** and **night**. As this happens, it seems to us that the Sun moves across the sky.

D The Earth *also* travels around the Sun in an **orbit**. It takes $365\frac{1}{4}$ days to complete one orbit. (365 days is 1 **year**). Every 4 years the four quarter days are added up to give us an extra day in February. This is a **leap year**.

E The Earth's axis is tilted which gives us **seasons**. In summer the **Northern hemisphere** points towards the Sun and so spends more time in sunlight. Days are longer in summer and so it is hotter. When it's summer in the UK it's winter in the **Southern hemisphere**.

FACT

The Arctic Circle is the area of the Northern hemisphere where, on one or more days each year, the Sun never rises.

Practice

1. Rewrite paragraph E to talk about what happens in winter.
2. What is:
   a an orbit
   b the axis of the Earth
   c a hemisphere of the Earth?

The Sun makes its own light and so is a **luminous source**. The **Moon** does not make its own light – it is a **non-luminous source**. However you can see the Moon because it **reflects** light from the Sun.

The Moon takes 28 days to orbit the Earth – a **lunar month**. As it travels around the Earth people on Earth can see less or more of its lit side and it looks as if the Moon changes shape. This is called the **phases of the Moon**.

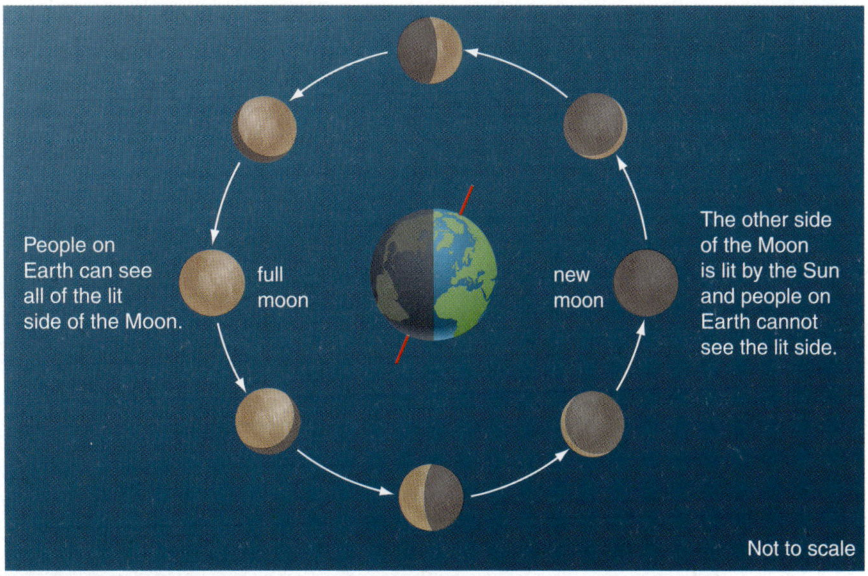

Sometimes the Moon gets between the Sun and the Earth. Its shadow falls on the Earth causing a **solar eclipse** (the sunlight is blocked and it goes dark).

A **lunar eclipse** is when the Earth's shadow falls on the Moon.

Write a list of all the words in bold on these two pages. Then go through them one at a time, making sure you can say what each one means.

3 a Why is it easy to see a full moon?

b Why is it hard to see a new moon?

c Draw out what the nine phases of the Moon look like from Earth, starting and ending with a new moon.

4 Street lights come on automatically at night time when it goes dark. Why do they come on during a solar eclipse?

5 Draw a diagram of a lunar eclipse. Remember the Earth is bigger than the Moon.

FACT The last total solar eclipse visible from the UK was in 1999.

How did I do?

	✔
I know why we have days, months and years.	☐
I know how we see the Sun and Moon.	☐

24: The Solar System

In this unit you will learn to answer these questions:

- What does the Solar System consist of?
- What is beyond the Solar System?

Use this mnemonic to remember the order of the planets from the Sun: My Very Easy Method Just Sums Up Names

Get started

Shut the book and write down as many words to do with the Solar System as you can think of.

The **Solar System** contains a **star** (the Sun), eight planets and a band of large rocks called the **asteroid belt**. There are also two dwarf planets, Pluto and Ceres (which is in the asteroid belt). The **asteroids** and the planets orbit the Sun.

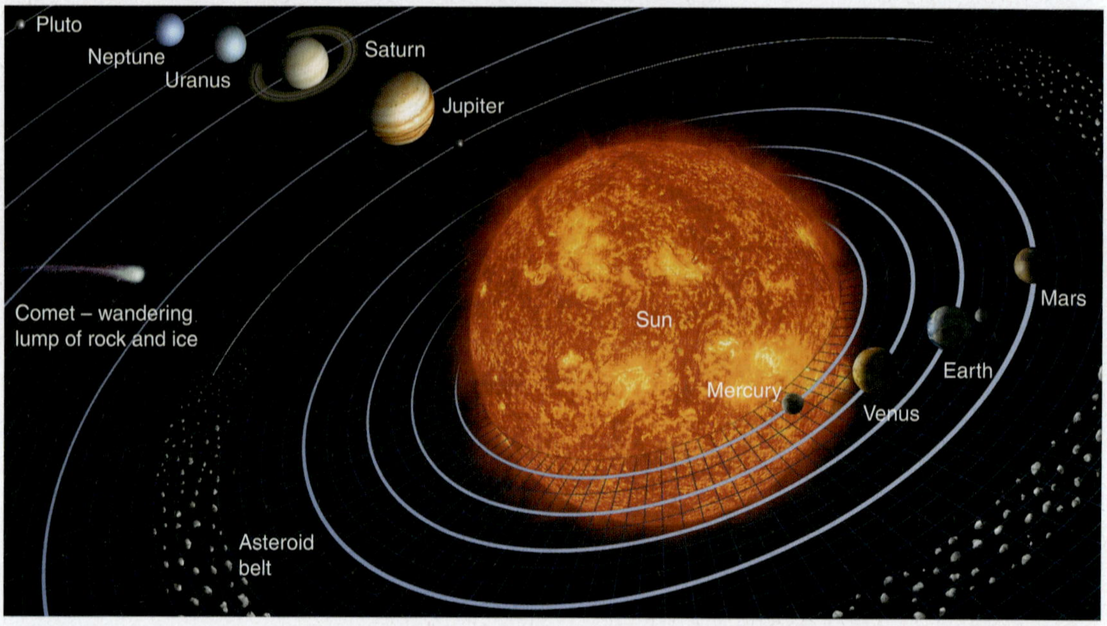

FACT There are over 100 000 other large (bigger than 50 km across) rocky objects beyond the orbit of Neptune in a region called the Kuiper belt. Pluto is in this belt.

Scientists find out about the Solar System by using **telescopes** or sending out **space probes** that send information back to Earth. The table shows some of the things we know about the other planets.

Planet	Time for 1 rotation	Time for 1 orbit	Distance from Sun (million km)	Mean surface temperature (°C)
Mercury	59 days	88 Earth days	58	170
Venus	243 days	224 Earth days	108	460
Earth	24 hours	365 Earth days	150	15
Mars	25 hours	687 Earth days	228	–50
Jupiter	10 hours	12 Earth years	778	–143
Saturn	10 hours	30 Earth years	1427	–195
Uranus	17 hours	84 Earth years	2871	–201
Neptune	16 hours	165 Earth years	4497	–220

Practice

1 Which planet has a day length most similar to Earth's?

2 How long does it take for Neptune to go once around the Sun?

3 a What do you notice about the temperatures of the planets as they get further from the Sun?
b Why do you think this is?

NASA image

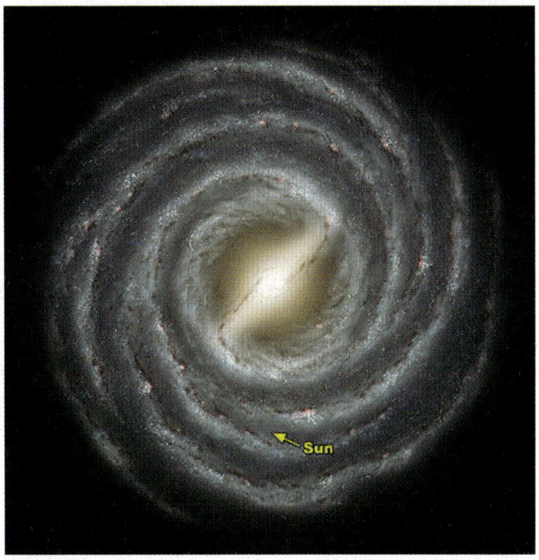

The Milky Way

Scientists think that for life to exist there must be liquid water, oxygen and a temperature that is not too hot or cold. Earth is the only place in the Solar System that has these conditions.

Outside the Solar System is the rest of the **Universe**. It contains billions of other stars that exist in huge clumps called **galaxies**. Our Sun is in a galaxy called the **Milky Way**.

Although stars are luminous sources, we can't see them during the day because the light from the Sun is so bright. We can see them at night though. Through history people have joined the stars with imaginary lines to form objects. Groups of stars linked in this way are called **constellations**.

Just as the Sun appears to move across the daytime sky as the Earth turns, so the stars appear to move across the night-time sky as the Earth turns.

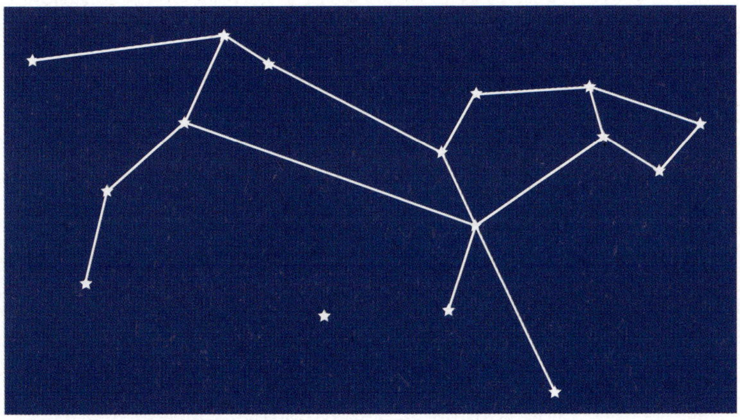

The constellation of Leo (a lion)

FACT Scientists measure distance in space using light years (the distance light travels in a year, which is 9.5 trillion km). Our closest star outside the Solar System is Proxima Centauri, which is 4.2 light years away.

4 What is the Milky Way?

5 Why do we think that Earth is the only place in the Solar System with life?

6 Why do constellations appear to move across the sky at night?

7 Think up four multiple-choice questions using the information on the last four pages. Try out your questions on someone else!

How did I do?

	✔
I know what the Solar System consists of.	☐
I know what is beyond the Solar System.	☐

Answers

1 Cells: Pages 8–9

Get started: The mains ones are: brain (controls the body), ear (hearing), eye (sight), gullet or foodpipe (taking food to stomach), heart (pumping blood), kidneys (cleaning the blood), large intestine (removes water from food), liver (making and destroying substances), lungs (breathing), skin (protection and feeling), small intestine (digesting food), stomach (digesting food), windpipe or trachea (taking air to and from lungs).

1 Check your list with the Glossary.
2 ×200
3 keeps a specimen flat and stops it drying out on a slide
4 your own answer
5 controls a cell's activities
6 supports and protects a plant cell
7 cytoplasm, nucleus, cell surface membrane
8 **a** See the diagram at the top of page 9.
b Plant cell, because it has a cell wall, a vacuole and chloroplasts.
9 Chloroplast, because all the others are found in both plants and animals (there are other correct answers!).
10 your own drawing with cytoplasm, cell surface membrane and nucleus labelled

2 What cells do: Pages 10–11

Get started: A neurone, B sperm cell, C ciliated epithelial cell

1 a group of cells of the same type
2 root
3 number of cells increases by cell division and cells get bigger
4 they are long to carry information a long way
5 **a** 300 grams of sugar per litre; **b** number of pollen tubes that grew in different sugar solutions (or something along those lines!); **c** so you can be sure that a result is right
6 **a** like one of the cells in the diagram on page 10 with labels; **b** It has a 'root hair' that provides more surface area for water to get into the cell.
7 ciliated epithelial tissue
8 diagram of cell division like the one on page 10

3 Reproduction: Pages 12–13

Get started: something like this:

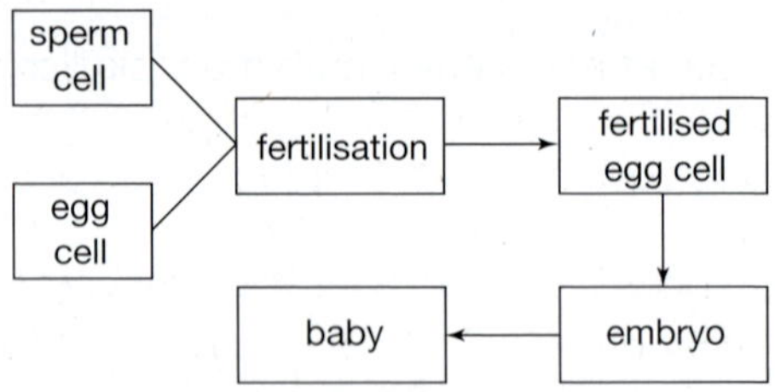

1 Ducks use internal fertilisation and goldfish use external fertilisation. Internal fertilisation is more likely to result in fertilised egg cells and ducks look after their young, so they need to produce fewer offspring to ensure that some survive.
2 uterus
3 **a** 3; **b** 28 October; **c** uterus lining passes out of vagina; **d** to make sure that if an embryo is formed it has a fresh lining
4 testes
5 **a** uterus – where the embryo/fetus/baby develops; **b** sperm duct – carries sperm cells from the testes to the urethra; **c** oviduct – carries egg cells from the ovary to the uterus

4 Growing up: Pages 14–15

Get started: something like this:

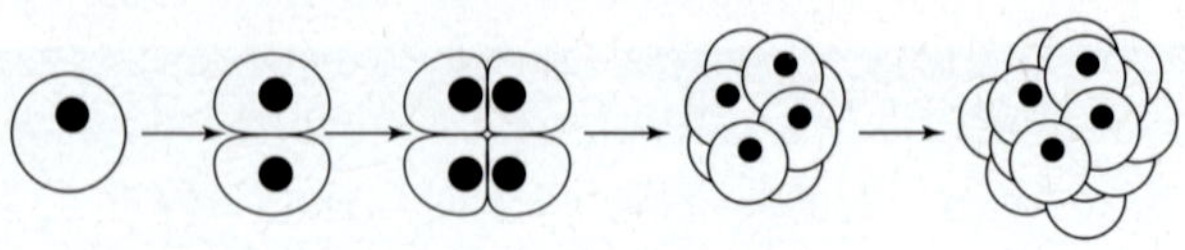

1 to feed it because it has no teeth
2 the uterus contracts
3 your own list
4 your own list
5 lungs → blood → placenta → umbilical cord → fetus's blood → fetus's brain
6 **a** chemicals made by the body that travel in the blood; **b** cause changes in the body
7 The sample size is too small.

5 Habitats: Pages 16–17

Get started: your own list – most organisms that live underground are tube-shaped to allow them to move easily through tunnels.

1 Your own creation but it should be able to keep warm!
2 hot during the day and cold at night, dry
3 camouflage to avoid being spotted by predators
4 Arctic, desert, ocean, underground, wood
5 Daily changes happen every day, seasonal changes occur slowly over the course of a year.
6 **a** seasonal change; **b** It helps to keep it warm in winter.
7 There's not much food about in winter.
8 swallow – but there are plenty of other examples
9 an investigation where only one thing (called a factor or variable) is changed

6 Feeding relationships: Pages 18–19

Get started: grass → rabbit → fox – make sure you get the arrows the right way round. If you've got this wrong try remembering that the arrow means 'is eaten by'.

1 sharp claws for catching prey, forward-facing eyes for good, 3D vision, sharp teeth to rip apart flesh, runs fast
2

rose bush	→	aphid	→	ladybird
producer		*consumer*		*consumer*
		herbivore		*carnivore*
		prey		*predator*

3 Any of four food chains:
bramble → wood mouse → stoat → fox
or bramble → wood mouse → stoat → owl
or grass → rabbit → stoat → fox
or grass → rabbit → stoat → owl.
4 how the energy goes from organism to organism/what eats what
5 stoats, wood mice, bank voles and dormice
6

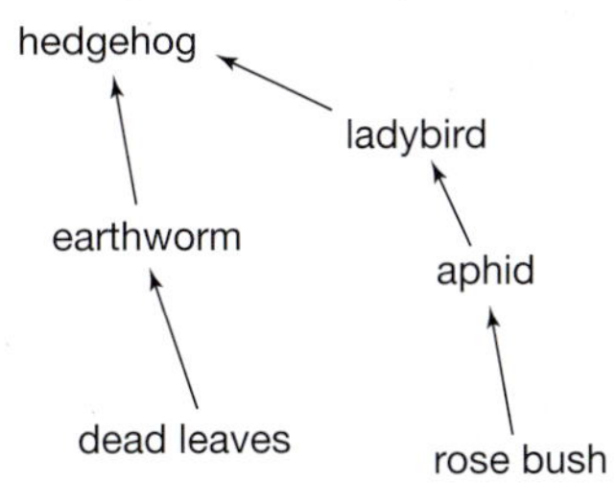

7 **a** Bank voles and dormice would have less to eat and some might starve. With fewer bank voles and dormice the owls would have to eat more wood mice and stoats and their populations might go down. **b** There would be less grass but the stoats and foxes would have more to eat and so more of them would survive. There are other answers to both parts **a** and **b** because all the organisms are connected together in a food web.
8 The stinging nettles sting their noses.

7 Variation: Pages 20–21

Get started: Tigers have stripes, lions don't; lions have tufted tails, tigers don't; tigers have white on their bellies, lions don't; tigers don't have manes, male lions do, tigers don't have tufted tails, lions do.

1 the differences between organisms
2 your own answers
3 **a** Do taller people have bigger hand widths? *or* Do smaller people have smaller hand widths? *or* Do taller people have smaller hand widths? *etc.*
b Taller people have bigger hand widths.
4 no
5 Mum (blond) and Dad (straight)
6 It is a small type of plant, it is a young plant, it has not had enough fertiliser, it has not had enough light, it has not had enough water, someone has cut it back – there are plenty of reasons!
7 Eye colour is the only inherited characteristic (but you might have another answer which would be correct).
8 your own drawing

8 Classification: Pages 22–23

Get started: Similarities – four limbs, hair, two eyes, body shape. Differences – bat has wings, bat has some limbs much longer than the others. When answering questions like this stick to things that you can see, because it's a much better way of classifying animals. Saying that bats fly is true but if you're trying to sort animals into groups of things that are most like each other you'll find that you end up putting bats with birds, when of course bats are mammals and not birds. The best way of telling these two animals apart is that bats have wings and hamsters don't.

1 **a** three body sections, six legs; **b** shape of antennae, pattern of stripes, colour of stripes
2 the largest groups that organisms are sorted into
3 body covering
4 on the basis of number of legs
5 animal kingdom, invertebrate, arthropod, insect
6 your own masterpiece!

9 Acids and alkalis: Pages 24–25

Get started: Acids are sour to taste, can be dangerous, have pHs below 7; alkalis feel soapy to the touch, can be dangerous, have pHs above 7.

1 Hydrochloric acid and car battery acid, but you could also have things like sulfuric acid and nitric acid.
2 to dilute the acid so it is less dangerous
3 The real one looks like this:

4 pH 3 (remember that you always spell pH with a small 'p' and a capital 'H')
5 weak acid
6 toilet cleaner or oven cleaner
7 a substance that changes colour depending on whether an acid or an alkali is added to it
8 **a** pH 7; **b** pure water
9 **a** it won't change its colour; **b** pale green
10 your own answers

10 Neutralisation: Pages 26–27

Get started: there are different ways of doing this but a good way is: car battery acid and oven cleaner (they are both strong but opposite. One is a strong acid and one is a strong alkali), orange juice and milk of magnesia (they are both weak), milk and seawater (they are both very weak). Have a look at the diagram of the pH scale on page 25 to help you see this.

1 when an acid cancels out an alkali
2 add an alkali
3 strong alkalis are dangerous
4 acidic, because an alkali (bicarbonate of soda) is needed to neutralise them
5 Super Tummy since the least amount was needed to raise the pH above pH 6
6 antacid tablets of the different types, measuring cylinder, universal indicator, hydrochloric acid, spatula, beaker or cup, stirrer or spoon, safety glasses
7 How quickly can different antacids neutralise an acid? How many tablets of different antacids are needed to neutralise an acid? How much in grams of different antacids are needed to neutralise an acid?

11 Simple chemical reactions: Pages 28–29

Get started: In the ice cube you can freeze the water to get ice back. You can never get back raw egg from cooked egg.

1 No new materials are made in a physical change (most chemical reactions are irreversible, but not all). In a chemical reaction new substances are formed.
2 a reaction occurs/a gas is given off
3 water → steam – physical change, the rest are chemical reactions
4 hydrogen (the other product is magnesium chloride – you will learn about this another time)
5 carbon dioxide (the other products are water and calcium sulphate – you will learn about this another time)
6 **a** It explodes with a squeaky pop when ignited. **b** It turns limewater milky.
7 It goes out because the gas produced is carbon dioxide.

12 Burning: Pages 30–31

Get started: Your labels should show that ash is made which cannot be turned back into wood, and that heat and light are given out which are both signs of a chemical reaction occurring.

1 A bright light and heat are given off and a new substance is formed.
2 Things burn better in 100% oxygen than in air which is only 20% oxygen.
3 calcium + oxygen → calcium oxide
4 something that contains a store of energy that can be changed into heat energy (usually when it is burned)
5 candle wax + oxygen → water + carbon dioxide
6 **a** The oxygen was used up. **b** The water took the place of the oxygen in the jar.
7 It cools the fire and takes away the heat (heat is one of the three things needed for combustion).
8 hydrogen + oxygen → water

13 Solids, liquids and gases: Pages 32–33

Get started: Solids – sand, stone, wood; liquids – milk, water; gases – air, carbon dioxide, hydrogen.

1 **a** solids and liquids; **b** solids; **c** gases
2 a scientific idea that can be used to explain observations and data
3 saying what will happen in an investigation
4 Water, air, hydrogen, milk – there's a huge list of things that it could be; all gases and liquids can flow.
5 tiny particles that you can't see

6 There are lots of different answers to this: a good point might be that there would be no harmful acids or alkalis; a bad point might be that there would be no milk to drink; an interesting fact might be that life cannot exist without water.

14 The particle theory: Pages 34–35

Get started: A grid of particles – always have a go at these Get started questions even if you're not sure if you're right – it will get your brain thinking in the right way!

1 **a** Magnesium is a solid, so:

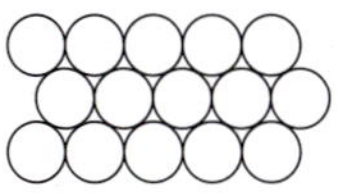

b Helium is a gas, so:

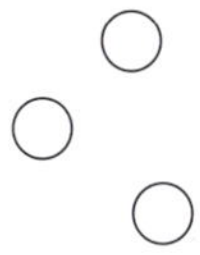

c Mercury is a liquid, so:

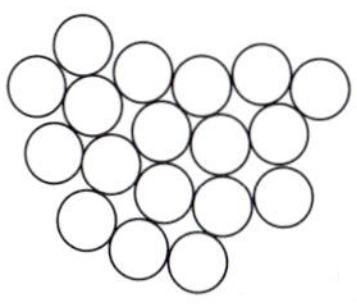

2 **a** When particles of a liquid or a gas spread through another liquid or gas. **b** When a solid breaks up into particles that spread out through a liquid so you can't see solid pieces any longer.
3 It dissolves.
4 The air pressure outside the tin pushes on the walls of the tin. There is no air inside the tin to push back, so the tin crumples.
5 Your drawing should look a bit like this:

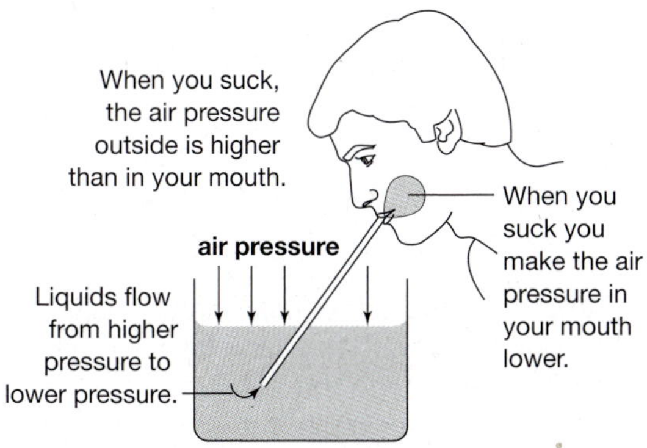

15 Solutions: Pages 36–37

Get started: There are lots of possible answers. The best one is probably salt because all the others are insoluble in water and salt is soluble in water.

1 different substances jumbled up together
2 salt, sugar
3 The rest of the mass was the mass of the rock.
4 320 g
5 **a** A solute dissolved in a solvent. **b** You can't see through it. **c** You could name any suspension, e.g. muddy water, mayonnaise, hand cream, blood, paint.
6 insoluble, soluble, solution, solute, solvent
7 condensation

16 More about dissolving: Pages 38–39

Get started: The only pure substance in the list is water, but remember that there are many different types of water (e.g. seawater, tap water, mineral water) and most of them are solutions. The only pure type of water is 'pure water' or 'distilled water'). The other liquids are all mixtures.

1 a substance made of only one material
2 **a** no; **b** The ink has separated into more than one colour. **c** ink D; **d** inks A and C
3 to check if there are things in it that should not be there
4 **a** a solution in which no more solute will dissolve; **b** Stir and add sugar until no more will dissolve and you can see undissolved sugar.
5 **a** sugar; **b** aspirin
6 **a** The solubility goes up. **b** 180 g/100 cm^3 of water; **c** On the graph, if you put a ruler along the line showing the solubility of salt, you will see that at 100 °C the line crosses at about 39 g/100 cm^3 of water or 40 g/100 cm^3 of water; so the solubility of salt at 100 °C is about 39 or 40 g/100 cm^3 of water.
7 The solubility of sugar is higher at hotter temperatures.
8 As the water cools the solubility of benzoic acid gets less and so not as much benzoic acid will dissolve in the water (some of the benzoic acid 'comes out of solution').

17 Fuels: Pages 40–41

Get started: coal, petrol, natural gas, diesel

1 light, heat
2 sizes and types of all apparatus, amount of fuel, time of burning
3 **a** paraffin – 20 °C, ethanol – 19 °C, wood – 12 °C, firelighter – 44 °C; **b** firelighter; **c** It produced the biggest change in temperature.
4 A fuel formed from the dead remains of prehistoric animals and plants.
5 plants die; plants are buried; plant remains are squashed and heated and turn into coal
6 dead, tiny sea animals and plants
7 It takes millions of years to form and so can't be made again.
8 your own design

18 Energy resources: Pages 42–43

Get started: Renewable – geothermal, Sun, water, wind, wood; non-renewable – coal, oil.

1 a fuel made from a living thing
2 The Sun doesn't shine at night.
3 your own design, but it should involve a renewable energy resource
4 food
5 **a** 1265 kJ; **b** 506 000 apples
6

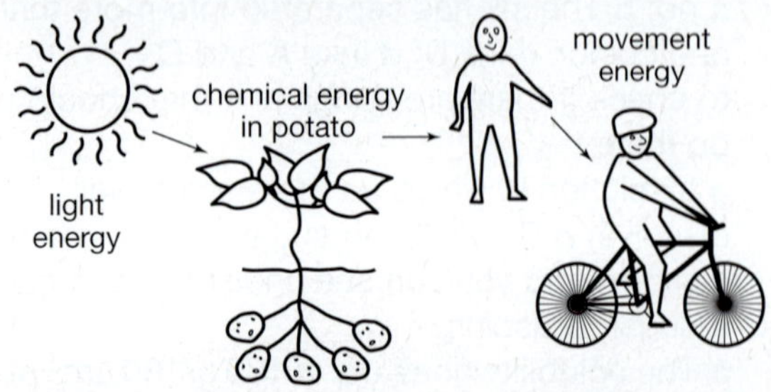

7 Use the apparatus shown on page 40 to burn the same mass of each breakfast cereal and measure the temperature rise of the water; the higher temperature rise would be given by the cereal with more energy.

19 Electrical circuits: Pages 44–45

Get started:

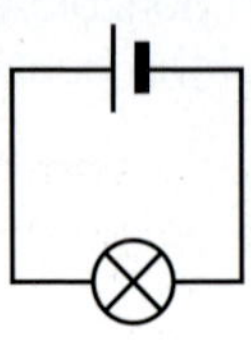

1 bulb/cell/resistor/switch
2 The switch is open so that there is a gap in the circuit.
3 **a**

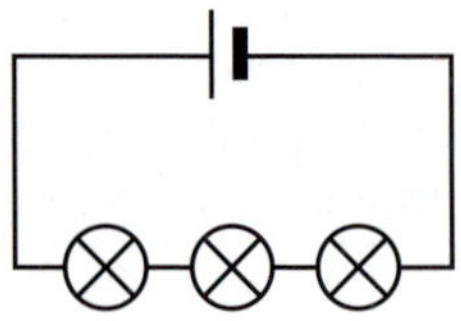

b dimmer/less bright
4

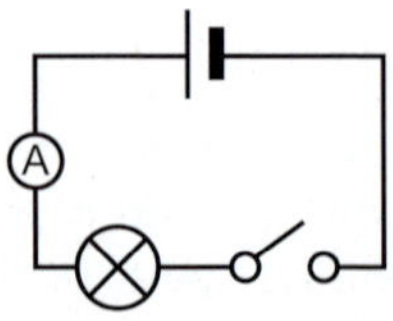

5 the 9 V cell
6 **a** plus end to minus end; **b** X – 2, Y – 3, Z – can't tell/lots

20 More circuits: Pages 46–47

Get started: Same diagram as for the Get started on page 44!

1 Another bulb can be added **in parallel**. Although each bulb slows the flow of current, there are now two routes for the current to take and so the current in the main part of the circuit flows faster.

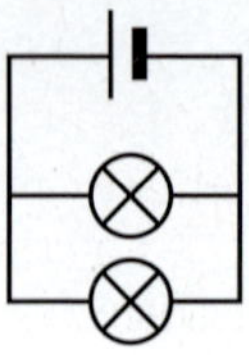

2 1 A
3 If you break a water pipe all the water flows out, but if you break a wire nothing flows out.
4 So that they all can be bright, or so that if one blows all the lights in the house don't go out.
5

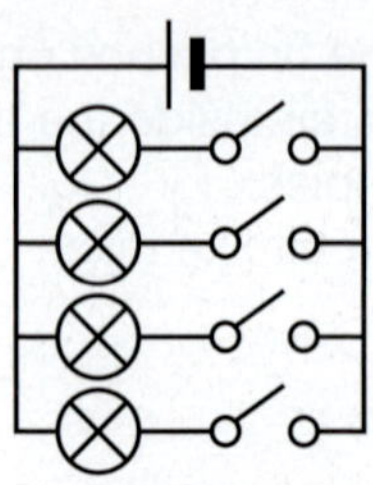

6 So that if something goes wrong and too much current flows through an appliance it doesn't catch fire.
7 **a** X – dimmer, Y – brighter, Z – normal (remember this is a parallel circuit – each loop has one bulb on it and each loop will allow the same current to go through it as if it were the only loop in the circuit); **b** L = 0.1 A (current does not get used up and is the same throughout a series circuit), M = 0.1 A, N = 0.9 A, O = 0.6 A, P = 0.3 A (the current divides to go down the different loops where the bulbs are and then joins up again)

21 Different forces: Pages 48–49

Get started:

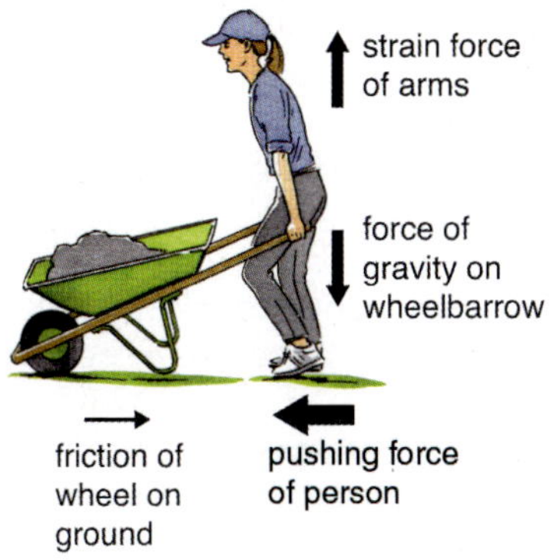

Don't worry if you didn't get all of these. Things to watch out for, though, are the fact that the arrows show not only the directions of forces but also their sizes – bigger arrow = bigger force.

1 **a** friction caused by something moving through air or water; **b** air resistance, water resistance
2 **a** a force that does not need to touch something to have an effect; **b** static electricity, magnetism, gravity
3 Your force arrow should point up and be labelled 'strain force' or 'force pulling up from forcemeter'.
4 forces that are equal in size and working in opposite directions
5 **a** To check that your measurements are right and you get reliable evidence. **b** If you double the weight you double the extension of the spring.

22 Weight and friction: Pages 50–51

Get started: A standard apple has a mass of about 100 g and so it has a weight of 1 N (newtons). Six apples weigh about 6 N.

1 **a** 10 N; **b** 5 N; **c** 2 kg
2 reducing friction by using a lubricant
3 **a** about 16 N; **b** the block, the forcemeter, the person pulling the block, the weight of the block
4 **a** 12 metres; **b** miles per hour
5 Rainwater acts as a lubricant on the road and reduces the friction between the tyres and the road, so increasing the time it takes to stop.
6 There is not as much friction on ice as there is on a normal road surface.
7 Friction stops your feet slipping and sliding and so allows you to walk.
8 Your own answers, e.g. friction is useful on the feet of a ladder on a pavement; it is not useful when you go on a slide.

23 Sun, Moon and Earth: Pages 52–53

Get started: Your diagram should show a light ray or light rays from the Sun being reflected by the Moon towards the Earth. Part of the diagram at the top of page 53 shows this. The Moon shines because it reflects sunlight.

1 The Earth's axis is tilted which gives us seasons. In winter the Northern hemisphere points away from the Sun and so spends more time in darkness. Days are shorter in winter and so it is colder. When it's winter in the UK it's summer in the Southern hemisphere.
2 **a** the path something takes around something else; **b** the imaginary line running through the Earth from pole to pole; **c** half of the Earth
3 **a** All of the side of the Moon facing us is sunlit and so it's very bright. **b** Most of the Moon's surface facing us is in darkness and so it's not very bright.
c

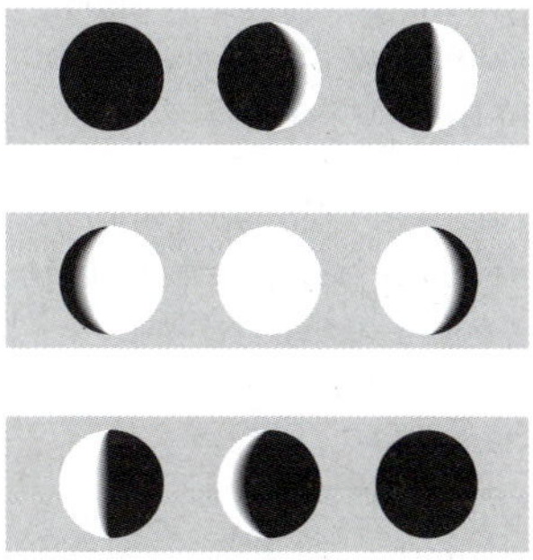

4 because it goes dark
5

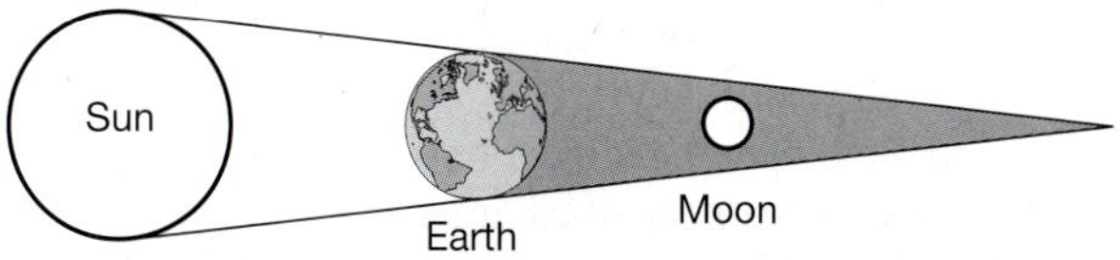

24 The Solar System: Pages 54–55

Get started: Your own list – have a look at all the words in bold on pages 52 to 55.

1 Mars
2 165 Earth years
3 **a** They get colder. **b** They are further from the heat of the Sun.
4 the galaxy that our Sun is in
5 It is the only body in the Solar System that has water, oxygen and a suitable temperature.
6 The Earth is rotating.
7 your own questions!

Glossary

abdomen Rear section of an insect body.
accuracy Correctness.
acid Liquid that has a pH of less than 7.
adaptation Features suited to a certain habitat.
adolescence When physical and emotional changes occur in teenagers.
afterbirth The placenta when pushed out after a birth.
air resistance Friction caused by things moving in air.
alkali Liquid that has a pH of more than 7.
ammeter Used to measure an electrical current.
amnion Bag that contains amniotic fluid.
amniotic fluid Liquid protecting a growing fetus.
amp Unit for electrical current (A).
amphibian Vertebrate with a body covered in moist skin.
antacid Weakly alkaline medicine to treat heartburn.
antennae Long parts on an insect used to sense things.
antibody Thing made by white blood cells that can destroy harmful bacteria and viruses.
arachnid Arthropod with eight legs and two body parts.
arthropod Invertebrate with jointed legs, a hard outer skeleton and a body divided into sections.
asteroid Lump of rock in space.
asteroid belt Area where there are lots of asteroids.
axis Imaginary line through Earth from pole to pole.
balanced forces When two forces on something are equal in size and opposite in direction.
bar chart Data shown as bars that vary in height.
battery Two or more electrical cells connected together.
biomass fuel Fuel made from a living thing.
bird Vertebrate with a body covered in feathers.
bladder Organ that stores urine.
bond Force that holds particles together.
braking distance The distance a car travels from when a driver presses the brake pedal until the car actually stops.
bulb Turns electrical energy into light energy.
Bunsen burner Used to heat things in a lab.
carbonate A type of chemical that reacts with acids to give off carbon dioxide gas.
carnivore Organism that only eats meat.
cell Basic building-block of all organisms.
cell division A cell splits to make two identical copies.
cell sap Liquid inside a plant cell vacuole.
cell surface membrane Thin covering of a cell.
cell wall Box that protects and supports plant cells.
cellulose Substance used to make plant cell walls.
centipede Arthropod with more than 14 jointed legs, one pair on each of many body sections.
cervix Ring of muscle that holds a fetus in the uterus.
characteristics What organisms look like.
chemical energy Energy stored in materials (e.g. food).
chemical reaction Change that makes new materials.
chlorophyll Green substance in chloroplasts.
chloroplast Green disc inside plant cells.
chromatogram The result of chromatography.
chromatography A way of separating different solutes.
cilia Hairs on some cells that sweep things along.
ciliated epithelial cells Cells with cilia on them.
classification Grouping organisms based on features.
coal Fossil fuel formed from dead plants.
combustion Scientific word for burning.
comet Lump of rock and ice that speeds through space.
complete circuit An electrical circuit with no gaps.
component Part in an electrical circuit (e.g. a bulb).
condensation Turning from a gas into a liquid.
constellation Imaginary grouping of stars.
consumer Organism that eats other organisms.
contact force Force that only exists when things touch.
contracts Gets smaller.
correlation Link between two things; so that if one thing is changed the other changes.
corrosion When a chemical reaction destroys something.
corrosive Will attack your body, especially your skin.
coverslip Thin piece of glass placed on a specimen.
current Flow of electricity.
cytoplasm Where new substances are made in a cell.
daily change Change in a habitat happening every day.
data Information obtained from investigations.
day When light from the Sun reaches part of the Earth. 'A day' is the time for the Earth to turn once on its axis.
density The mass of 1 cm^3 of a substance.
diffusion The natural spreading of particles of a liquid or a gas through another liquid or gas.
dilution Adding water to something.
dissolving The breaking up of a solid in a liquid.
distillation Evaporation followed by condensation.
drag Friction caused by things moving in gases or liquids.
Earth The 3rd planet from the Sun in the Solar System.
echinoderm Invertebrate with a body in five parts.
ecologist A scientist who investigates habitats.
egg cell Female sex cell.
electric shock Pain caused by electricity flowing in you.
electrical energy An energy that is carried through wires connected to cells.
embryo Clump of cells that grow into a new organism.
energy resource Thing used to produce useful energy.
environment Conditions in a habitat (e.g. temperature).
environmental variation A characteristic that has been caused by something in the surroundings.
equator Imaginary line around the middle of the Earth.
evaporation Turning from a liquid into a gas.
eyepiece lens The microscope lens you look through.
fair test An investigation when you only change one thing.
feeding relationship Way in which one organism depends on another for food.
female reproductive system All the organs that are used for reproduction in females.
fertilisation When sex cells join together (or fuse).
fertilised egg cell What is formed during fertilisation.
fetus An embryo that has developed arms and legs.
filter 'A filter' is something used to separate insoluble substances from a liquid. 'To filter' is to use a filter.
fish Vertebrate with a body covered in wet scales.
flammable Will easily catch fire.
flower Plant organ that makes seeds.
focusing wheel Wheel used to focus a microscope.
food chain A diagram showing what eats what.
food web A diagram made of many food chains.
fossil fuel A fuel formed from dead organisms.
friction A contact force that pulls back on things sliding past each other.
fuel Substance that can be made to give out heat energy.
full moon When we can see all the lit side of the Moon.
function Another word for a 'job'.
fuse Contains a wire that melts if too much current flows.

fuse (biology) To join together.
galaxy Group of millions of stars in space.
gas State of matter. Gases flow, take up the shapes and volumes of their containers and can be squashed.
generator It produces electrical energy as it turns.
geothermal power Electricity produced when water is turned to steam underground and used to turn a turbine.
gestation The time between fertilisation and birth.
glands Pockets in the body that produce liquids.
gravity Force that exists between any two things, pulling them together (e.g. the Earth and you).
habitat Area where organisms live (e.g. sea, woodland).
harmful Will damage a part of your body.
hazard symbol Drawing that warns about dangerous chemicals.
head Front section of an insect body.
heart Organ that pumps blood.
heat energy Hot things contain more heat energy.
hemisphere Half the Earth.
herbivore Organism that only eats plants.
hibernation Going to sleep for the winter.
hormone Chemical made in your body that causes changes.
hydroelectric power Electricity produced when water flows out of a reservoir and turns turbines.
implantation When an embryo sticks in the uterus lining.
inherited Characteristics passed from parents to offspring.
inherited variation Characteristic inherited from a parent.
insect Arthropod with six legs and three body parts.
insoluble Something that does not dissolve.
invertebrates Animals that don't have backbones.
irreversible change Change which cannot be reversed.
irritant Will make a part of your body hurt.
joule The unit for energy (J).
Jupiter 5th planet from the Sun in the Solar System.
kilojoule One thousand joules (kJ).
kinetic energy Another name for movement energy.
kingdoms Largest groups living things are sorted into.
leaf Plant organ that makes food.
leap year A year on Earth in which an extra day is added.
light energy The energy produced by luminous sources.
limewater Clear, colourless liquid that goes 'milky' when carbon dioxide is added.
line graph Data shown as a line going through points.
line of best fit Straight line that goes the best way through all the points on a line graph.
liquid Liquids flow, take up the shapes of their containers, keep their volumes, cannot be squashed.
litmus Indicator. Turns red in acids and blue in alkalis.
lubricant Something that reduces friction.
luminous source Something that produces its own light.
lunar eclipse When the Earth blocks light from the Sun reaching the Moon.
lunar month Time for the Moon to orbit the Earth once.
magnetism The force between two magnets or a magnet and a magnetic material.
magnify To make something appear bigger.
mains electricity The electricity that flows to our homes.
male reproductive system All the organs that are used for reproduction in males.
mammal Vertebrate with a body covered in hair.
Mars 4th planet from the Sun in the Solar System.
mass The amount of matter in something.
menstrual cycle Cycle in women that causes egg cells to be released and the uterus lining to be replaced.
menstruation The passing of the lining of the uterus out through the vagina in women.
Mercury Planet closest to the Sun in our Solar System.
methane The gas found in natural gas.
microscope It magnifies small things.
migration Going to another place for a season.
Milky Way The galaxy that our Sun is in.
millipede Arthropod with more than 14 jointed legs, two pairs on each of many body sections.
mixture Different substances jumbled up together.
model Familiar thing that can be used to think about what happens in an unfamiliar thing.
mollusc Invertebrate with a single fleshy muscle to move.
moon A rocky sphere that orbits the Earth.
movement energy Also called kinetic energy. Things that are moving have movement energy.
muscle tissue Lots of muscle cells grouped together.
natural gas A fossil fuel formed when oil forms.
Neptune The furthest planet from the Sun.
nerve cell Another name for a neurone.
neurone Cell that carries information around the body using electrical impulses.
neutral Liquid that has a pH of 7.
neutralisation When an acid and an alkali cancel out.
new moon When we cannot see the lit side of the Moon.
newton Unit for force (N).
night When sunlight is not reaching a part of the Earth.
nocturnal Active at night.
non-contact force Force that works even if two things aren't touching.
non-luminous source Something that does not produce its own light.
non-renewable Energy resource that cannot be remade.
North pole The top of the northern hemisphere.
Northern hemisphere Half the Earth above the equator.
nucleus Controls a cell.
nutrients Food substances that give you energy and keep you healthy.
nutrition information Label showing what is in a food.
objective lens Microscope lens closest to the specimen.
observation To look carefully at something.
offspring Young organisms produced by parents.
oil Fossil fuel formed from small dead sea organisms.
orbit The path of something around another thing.
organ Different tissues grouped together.
organism Living thing.
ovary Part of a female that produces egg cells.
oviduct Tube that carries egg cells towards the uterus.
ovulation When an ovary releases an egg cell.
ovule Bag that contains an egg cell in a flower.
parallel Circuit where each electrical component is connected on its own loop of wire.
particle theory Idea that all matter is made of tiny, moving particles.
peat Fossil fuel that can turn into coal.
penis Male organ used to put semen into a female.
pH scale Scale of strengths of acids and alkalis.
phases of the Moon Series of shapes caused by us seeing different amounts of the sunlit side of the Moon.

photosynthesis Process that plants use to make food.
physical change Change in which no new materials are made.
physical environmental factor Non-living feature of a habitat (e.g. temperature, amount of rain).
placenta Disc that takes oxygen and food from a mother's blood to give to a developing fetus. It passes the fetus's waste back to the mother's blood.
Pluto A dwarf planet in the Solar System.
pole The top or bottom of the Earth.
pollen grain Male sex cell in plants.
pollen tube Tube that grows from a pollen grain.
pollination When a pollen grain lands on a stigma.
population The number of a certain organism in a habitat.
predator Animal that eats other animals.
prediction What you think will happen in an investigation.
premature Early.
pressure The push on a certain area caused by a force.
prey Animal that is eaten by other animals.
producer Organism that makes its own food.
products The materials made by a chemical reaction.
puberty Time when physical changes occur in teenagers.
pure When a substance is made of only one material.
reactants The materials before a chemical reaction.
reflection When light bounces off a surface.
renewable An energy resource that will not run out.
reproduction When new organisms are created.
reptile Vertebrate with a body covered in dry scales.
resistance A property that slows down electric current.
reversible change Change which can be reversed so that you can get back the materials that you started with.
rock salt Mixture of rock and salt mined from the ground.
root Plant organ that takes in water and anchors a plant.
root hair cell Plant cell that is adapted to absorb water quickly from the ground by having a finger-like extension.
root hair tissue Lots of root hair cells grouped together.
sample size The number of measurements of the same type taken in an investigation.
saturated solution Solution that can dissolve no more solute.
Saturn 6th planet from the Sun in the Solar System.
scatter graph Data shown as points on a graph.
scrotal sac Bag of skin that holds the testes.
season Time of year when the weather behaves in a certain way.
seasonal change Habitat change that occurs each year.
seed Contains an embryo that grows into a new plant.
semen Mixture of sperm cells and fluids.
series Circuit where electrical components are connected one after the other along one wire.
sex cell Cell used to create a new organism.
sexual reproduction Reproduction that needs a male sex cell and a female sex cell.
slide A piece of glass on which a specimen is put.
solar cell Converts light energy into electrical energy.
solar eclipse When the Moon blocks light from the Sun reaching the Earth.
solar panel Panel containing tubes of water that heat up from the Sun.
Solar System The Sun, planets, moons and asteroids.
solid Solids don't flow, keep their shapes, keep their volumes, cannot be squashed.
solubility How much solute can dissolve in a certain amount of a liquid.
soluble Something that dissolves in a liquid.
solute Solid that dissolves in a solvent.
solution Solute dissolved in a solvent.
solvent Liquid part of a solution. Will dissolve a solute.
South pole The bottom of the southern hemisphere.
Southern hemisphere Half the Earth below the equator.
space probe Machine sent into space to explore.
species Members of the same species can breed with each other, members of different species can't.
specimen Object that you look at using a microscope.
sperm cell Male sex cell in animals.
sperm duct Tube carrying sperm cells out of the testes.
stage Area where a slide is placed on a microscope.
star Gigantic ball of fire in space.
states of matter The three different forms of materials – solid, liquid or gas.
static electricity Force that attracts things with electrical charges towards each other.
stem Plant organ that supports a plant and carries water.
stigma Female part of a flower that receives pollen.
stopping distance The distance a car travels from when a driver sees the need to stop until the car actually stops.
strain force Force in thing that is stretched or squashed.
streamlined Smooth shape that reduces drag.
style Female flower part down which a pollen tube grows.
Sun Our nearest star.
suspension Tiny insoluble pieces floating in a liquid.
switch Component that makes or closes a gap in a circuit.
symbol Easy-to-draw diagram used to show something.
telescope Device used to magnify distant objects.
testis Organ that makes sperm cells. (Plural is testes.)
theory Scientific idea used to explain data.
thinking distance The distance a car travels from when a driver thinks about stopping until the brake is pressed.
thorax Middle section of an insect's body.
tissue Lots of the same type of cell grouped together.
turbine Something that spins a generator.
universal indicator Liquid or papers that change colour depending on the pH.
Universe Everything in the whole of space.
upthrust A force that water pushes up with.
Uranus 7th planet from the Sun in the Solar System.
ureter Tube carrying urine into the kidneys.
urethra Tube carrying urine out of a body.
uterus Female organ where an embryo grows.
vacuole 'Bag' inside a plant cell for support and storage.
vagina Female organ where the penis is placed during sex.
variation The differences between living things.
Venus 2nd planet from the Sun in the Solar System.
vertebrates Animals that have backbones.
volt The unit for voltage (V).
voltage The amount of 'pushing power' that makes a current flow around a circuit.
volume The amount of space that something takes up.
water resistance Friction caused by things moving in water.
weight The force of the Earth's gravity on something.
word equation Shows the reactants in a chemical reaction followed by an arrow pointing to the products.
year The length of time a planet takes to orbit the Sun.